LAPTOP

FROM

HELL

HUNTER BIDEN, BIG TECH, AND THE DIRTY SECRETS
THE PRESIDENT TRIED TO HIDE

MIRANDA DEVINE

Post Hill
PRESS

A LIBERATIO PROTOCOL BOOK
An Imprint of Post Hill Press
ISBN: 978-1-63758-105-6
ISBN (eBook): 978-1-63758-106-3

Laptop from Hell:
Hunter Biden, Big Tech, and the Dirty Secrets the President Tried to Hide
© 2021 by Miranda Devine
All Rights Reserved

Cover photo taken August 3, 2018, at Palms Casino Resort, Las Vegas.

Post Hill Press
New York • Nashville
posthillpress.com

Published in the United States of America
4 5 6 7 8 9 10

To Col

CONTENTS

"Corruption is a cancer, a cancer that eats away at a citizen's faith in democracy.... It saps the collective strength and resolve of a nation. Corruption is just another form of tyranny."
—Joe Biden, Kyiv, Ukraine, 2014

In the spring of 2019, four years after the death of his brother Beau, Hunter Biden was falling apart.

His crack addiction was raging, his wife of twenty-four years had divorced him, his steamy affair with Beau's widow, Hallie, was on the rocks.

A stripper from Arkansas had launched a paternity suit. His business partners were in jail or had vanished, presumed dead. The fortune he had made from foreign oligarchs and Delaware donors was squandered or inaccessible.

He had spent the past year in and out of rehab, flitting between Airbnbs and the Chateau Marmont, unappreciated and disrespected, raging at his family and the world.

In April, his father, former vice president Joe Biden, announced he was running for president.

Two weeks later, Hunter left his laptop at a Mac repair shop in Delaware and never came back.

———◦•◦———

At its heart, this is the story of a son of political privilege tormented by the defining tragedy of his childhood.

In 1972, when Hunter was two, his mother, Neilia Hunter Biden, took the children on a Christmas shopping expedition near the family's home outside Wilmington, Delaware, when their car was struck by a truck. Neilia and Hunter's baby sister, Ashley, were killed. Hunter and his three-year-old brother, Beau, were injured and spent more than a month in hospital.

Their father, Joe, who always had aspired to lead the sort of sprawling Catholic dynasty embodied by the Kennedy clan, now was living through a Kennedy kind of tragedy.

Only a month earlier, he had won a coveted US Senate race in Delaware, becoming, at thirty, one of the youngest senators in American history.

He couldn't give that up, could he? So, he dried his tears and took the oath of office in the hospital room where his two motherless boys lay, Hunter with head injuries and Beau with a broken leg. Then he left his sons in the care of their aunt Val and went to work in Washington. Most nights he made the three-hour Amtrak commute home to kiss his sleeping children.

"The first memory I have is of lying in a hospital bed next to my brother," said Hunter, in a eulogy at Beau's funeral in 2015.

"I was almost three years old. I remember my brother—one year and one day older than me—holding my hand, staring into my eyes, saying, 'I love you. I love you. I love you.'"

The black and white images of two small, bandaged boys lying in a hospital bed, as their father was sworn in as a US senator in the background, captured a nation's heart. The photos have paid off politically for Biden ever since.

As he rose in politics, the story would be the lead anecdote of every profile, endearing him to voters and defining him as a heroic father figure.

Time and again, the sympathy it elicited helped shield "Quid Pro Joe" from criticism. Ultimately, the terrible blow only made him stronger.

His younger son, however, never would fully recover.

After the funeral mass for the brother he idolized, Hunter would recall in a note to himself: "I went to kneel in the back pew with my Dad…and I said my prayer, and for the first time in my life I prayed to, not just my dead mother and my dead sister, but also to my dead brother, and for the first time in my life I prayed for me.

"I asked, 'please let me be with you, please let me know you love me, please never let me forget, please let me come.'"

Introduction: October Surprise

> *"Character is on the ballot."*
> **—Joe Biden, February 2020**

Less than a month before the 2020 election, I was at home in midtown Manhattan, a few blocks from the *New York Post* newsroom, where I worked as a columnist, when my cell phone pinged at 11:35 p.m.

Rudy Giuliani's lawyer, Bob Costello, had sent a text message from his Long Island home: "I have been asked to send you a small taste of evidence that I have quite legally, that you might have an interest in," he wrote.

"I have approximately 40,000 emails, at least a thousand text messages and hundreds of photographs and videos involving the subject...

"The story is more about the emails, but the photos set the tone."

What followed were three startling images.

The first showed Hunter Biden, then aged forty-seven, still handsome but haggard, in bed, lighting what appeared to be a crack pipe.

Another showed Hunter asleep with the unlit pipe in his mouth.

The last photo was a half-naked selfie of Hunter in a bathroom mirror, showing a fresh tattoo across his tanned upper back, still covered in plastic wrap, long angry markings as if a tiger had clawed his flesh.

In fact, Hunter had just had the entire map of the Finger Lakes in upstate New York etched into his back. This was the place where his late mother, Neilia, had grown up, where he had forged some of his happiest childhood memories, during long summers with his maternal grandparents, the Scotch Presbyterian Hunters, at their cottage on Owasco Lake.

Hunter felt such a connection to the area that he named his various ill-fated companies after local landmarks, such as Owasco, Seneca, and Skaneateles.

The photographs were prima facie evidence that Costello and Giuliani had in their possession an extraordinary trove of material that already may have exposed the son of the man who would become president to blackmail and extortion by America's enemies.

Giuliani was a valuable source of information if you were a journalist in New York. The irrepressible seventy-six-year-old former mayor had the inside story on everything from the city's criminal history to the current mood in the Oval Office.

Once a crusading young DA for the Southern District of New York who took down the Mob in the 1980s, then the crime-busting mayor who cleaned up New York in the 1990s, he had mellowed into the eccentric, scotch-swilling consigliere for President Donald Trump.

Giuliani had been sent a copy of the contents of Hunter Biden's laptop by the owner of the Mac repair shop in Delaware where it had been abandoned.

The material will "blow your mind," said the former mayor.

Photographs of Hunter's rampant drug use and explicit homemade pornography were all over the laptop. But the real news value lay in the corporate documents, bank transfers, and emails detailing a vast international influence-peddling scheme, sanctioned by the world's most despotic regimes—and implicating "Honest Joe" Biden himself.

It would provide a window onto the corruption that is Washington's original sin, as conducted on a global scale by one of its most skilled and calculating practitioners.

The sordid secret vices of a son of political privilege were an incongruous backdrop to the monumental oil and gas deals Hunter was mixed up in around the world, a drug-addled neophyte bumbling through geopolitical minefields, with the Secret Service in tow.

Hunter's encounters with cutthroat oligarchs in Monte Carlo, Lake Como, Hong Kong, and Shanghai are documented in rich detail on his laptop. It takes us from a billionaire's beach villa in Acapulco to the desolate oil fields of Kazakhstan, from a judo competition in Budapest with Vladimir Putin to dinner in Beijing with Xi Jinping.

A Chinese tycoon cooks Hunter dinner in his new $50 million Manhattan penthouse, a Ukrainian oligarch takes him to his fishing shack in Norway. Beautiful Russian escorts and thieving drug dealers float through his self-imposed exile on Sunset Boulevard amid slapstick scenes as crack-head Hunter comes unstuck and his hapless Uncle Jim Biden rides in to the rescue.

Text messages chronicling the disintegration of Hunter's love affair with his brother's widow are laced with flashbacks to the pain of a troubled childhood.

Eye-popping financial windfalls are shaded by the grim fate of business partners who wind up floating in the Yangtze. It's a life of greed and luxury in a shadowy world of kleptocrat oligarchs that law enforcement can't touch.

Despite his secret debaucheries, Hunter was acutely aware of what he brought to the table: access to his powerful father.

This was the Biden family business, involving the president's brothers as well as Hunter, and it is documented in minute detail in the eleven-gigabyte trove. Over nine years from 2010 to 2019, the laptop shadows Joe's life as the globe-trotting vice president of the Obama administration, the favor-trading senator from Delaware who would go on to become leader of the free world.

The laptop also puts the lie to President Biden's repeated claims that he knew nothing about his son's shady business ventures in China, Ukraine, Kazakhstan, Russia, and beyond.

———— •••• ————

Five days after Costello's late-night call, on Wednesday, October 14, 2020, the *New York Post* published the first of a series of front-page bombshells, written by Emma-Jo Morris and Gabrielle Fonrouge, culled from the contents of Hunter's laptop.

The story, headlined "Biden's Secret Emails," revealed a bombshell 2015 email indicating that Joe, as vice president, had met in Washington with a high-ranking representative of the corrupt Ukrainian energy company that was paying his junkie son a million dollars a year to sit on its board.

Eight months after the meeting, Joe flew to Kyiv and threatened to withhold $1 billion in US aid unless the Ukrainian government fired its top prosecutor, Viktor Shokin, who was pursuing Burisma for corruption at the time.

The email was news, in anyone's language.

But soon after the *Post*'s story broke online, social media censored it. Facebook announced it had throttled the story's reach. Twitter locked the *Post*'s account for two weeks, then admitted after the election that it had made a mistake.

It was a chilling exercise of raw political power by an unaccountable Big Tech—the term given to the oligopoly of global corporations that dominate the information technology industry.

The coordinated censorship of America's oldest newspaper, with the fourth largest circulation in the nation, amounted to election interference.

It was a historic moment that rang alarm bells around the world and would harden resolve on Capitol Hill to rein in the power of the social media giants.

Polls suggest that if the full story of the Bidens' international influence-peddling scheme had been told before the election it could have changed votes in crucial marginal seats and possibly flipped the result.

I have authenticated material on the laptop by interviewing, on background, several recipients of Hunter's emails and messages. A collection of documents obtained from Hunter's former business partner Tony Bobulinski, including WhatsApp messages with Hunter and Jim Biden, crossmatches with material on the laptop.

Overseas payments into bank accounts linked to Hunter and his associates, which were detailed by the Senate Republican inquiry into Hunter, provided additional context to bank statements and tax documents on the laptop. Filling in the gaps were confidential "suspicious activity reports" that banks are required to flag to the Treasury Department.

Another point of light came from investigative journalists Peter Schweizer and Matthew Tyrmand who shared with me some of the material they were given by one of Hunter's jailed former business partners, Bevan Cooney.

Corroborated from multiple angles, Hunter's laptop tells an alarming story of the national interest sold out for personal gain at the highest level, in particular to Communist China, our greatest strategic foe.

The conclusion is inescapable. The president cannot extricate his family's moneymaking schemes from America's foreign policy imperatives.

—New York, June 2021

CHAPTER

1

A Knock at the Door

"He is the smartest man I know."
—President Joe Biden on Hunter, CBS News, 2020

Hunter Biden was in the sixth week of a crack cocaine bender at the Chateau Marmont in May 2018, paying hookers and dealers to service him around the clock in an $820 a night garden cottage by the hotel pool, a few steps from the bungalow where John Belushi had died thirty-six years earlier from a heroin speedball.

He was flush with cash, having wound up his business with the Chinese energy company CEFC after the sudden disappearance in Shanghai in March of his billionaire partner, chairman Ye Jianming, and the arrest at JFK airport four months earlier of Patrick Ho, another Chinese partner who would end up in jail for paying bribes to African presidents at the United Nations.

Hunter's playboy lifestyle at the time included a $650-per-day Lamborghini Gallardo Spyder from Legends Car Rentals, which he drove around town until his Porsche 911 was delivered by a valet driver from where he'd left it in a parking lot at Dulles airport in Washington, DC.

The legendary Chateau Marmont, on Sunset Strip in Hollywood, was an oasis of celebrity discretion and distressed décor, where Hunter liked to retreat after financial windfalls and relationship breakdowns.

He indulged his appetites in the style of Pan, the lecherous half-man, half-goat, chaser of nymphs, symbol of lust from Greek mythology, whose image features in the hotel logo.

He learned to cook crack over the four-burner stove in the tiny cottage kitchen, as he recounts in his memoir, weighing the white rocks in baggies on "Cheech and Chong" scales and photographing them.

He would call escorts with Eastern European names to make house calls: "Hi, This is Rob. I'm staying at Chateau Marmont. Are you available now?"

Day after day he smoked crack, drank vodka, made porn videos. One time he balanced a line of M&Ms on his erect penis and took photographs of it.

He would periodically move out of the Chateau for a few days to another hotel nearby, The Jeremy or La Peer.

But wherever he went, crisis followed "Johnny Drama," as his sister-in-law turned lover, Hallie, used to describe Hunter to friends behind his back.

One overcast spring day in L.A., Hunter is catching up on porn. He spends $1,000 from one of his Wells Fargo debit cards to top up his account on the sex-cam site STREAMRAY, where women with names such as PerfectTits and SamanthaSquirt take off their clothes and writhe around live on camera for money.

Annoyingly, Wells Fargo keeps sending alerts saying he's tripped his credit card limit of $65,000.

He's not been answering his phone, but the bills are piling up and Uncle Jim Biden and wife, Sara, keep hassling him for money. They resend their May invoice of $82,500, for "monthly retainer for international business development."

Hunter emails Edward Prewitt, his Wells Fargo wealth adviser: "Please Wire $99,000 to Jim Biden's account today please and please transfer $75,000 to me."

That should keep everyone off his back for a while.

Now Hunter is fuming as he pores over last month's transactions at the Cathay Bank's New York branch for one of his firms, Hudson West III, into which $5 million of Chinese money had been funneled before Ho's arrest the previous year.

Hunter squints at the bank statement. The balance shows $1 million in a money market account and $520,000 in a checking account. But what is this $2 million debit from March 16?

Hunter circles the number and scrawls "What???" He adds his initials, pressing hard into the paper, and writes "why" in a childish hand, underlining the word several times. Then he photographs the page.

What the hell. Time for fun.

He trawls through his favorite L.A. escort websites and orders "Yanna" (not her real name), a twenty-four-year-old Russian native from Emerald Fantasy Girls, who at least speaks English, unlike some of the others, which always annoys him when it comes time to pay.

"Russian, Green Eyes, Thin Brunette, an elite courtesan" is Yanna's pitch, along with a menu of sex acts, none of which is off limits.

Hunter's escapades with Yanna, in his $469 room at The Jeremy, are a glimpse into the debauched lifestyle of the president's son but also raise questions about how much his finances were mingled with Joe's.

One day bleeds into the next, and then Yanna wants to be paid. The problem is Hunter's debit cards aren't working and she's not leaving without the $8,000 he owes her for the extended callout.

On the morning of May 24, hungover and out of sorts, Hunter adds a new recipient on the cash transfer app Zelle, the registered agent for Emerald Fantasy Girls. He transfers $8,000. It doesn't work. A few minutes later, Wells Fargo sends him a fraud detection alert.

He reaches into his wallet, pulls out a card, and transfers the $8,000, but it doesn't go through. He rifles through his wallet again: "Try this one." No luck. He pulls out another card. Bingo.

Yanna leaves, and he crashes. But while he sleeps, his bank accounts are being emptied. In receipts he saves on the computer, the transactions he thought had failed have gone through, one after the other.

The first $8,000 is recorded leaving his account at 10:22 a.m. At 10:50 a.m., $2,000 leaves a different account. At 10:59 a.m., $3,500 vanishes. At 11:00 a.m., another $8,000. At 11:03 a.m., another $3,500. About $25,000 moves in under an hour. Another $3,500 is scheduled to transfer out later that afternoon but will be delayed.

Soon enough, his cell phone starts pinging. It's Yanna: "There is many transactions on my account," she texts. "From last night 8k, 8k, 3500k. So get back with me when you can. So I can transfer back to you. Better if you call my personal."

She follows up: "I'm happy to see that much in my account."

Her last text: "No worries you can have the rest back. Karma is a bitch."

Hunter's curt reply at 4:19 p.m: "Send it back please."

Text messages indicate most of the money was returned over the next week. But on June 12, Yanna texted Hunter that she could not transfer the remaining $5,000 because of problems with her bank account.

"Bullshit," replied Hunter. "I am so sick of this."

What happens between Hunter and Yanna next is not recorded. Yanna's private cell phone number no longer works, and Emerald Fantasy Girls is defunct.

What we do know from the laptop is that a few hours after Hunter's debit-card woes began, two former Secret Service agents will show up at the hotel, asking curious questions.

Text messages start arriving from a man named "Rob" who is listed in Hunter's contacts as being from the Secret Service's Los Angeles field office. We will not give his full name for legal reasons, but Rob's phone number and Secret Service email address appear on the laptop, with a photographic avatar and the description "USSS Special Agent in Charge."

The Secret Service says Rob retired from the agency on April 30, 2018—a little over three weeks before Hunter's L.A. binge—and that the agency "did not provide protection to any member of the Biden family in 2018."

Hunter's laptop features a message from Rob on May 24 at 6:37 p.m.

"H—I'm in the lobby come down. Thanks, Rob."

Hunter replies: "5 minutes."

Five minutes later Rob texts again: "Come on H, this is linked to Celtic's [Joe Biden's] account.

"DC is calling me every 10. Let me up or come down. I can't help if you don't let me H."

"Celtic" was Joe Biden's Secret Service code name when he was vice president.

Did one of the credit cards used to pay Yanna belong to Joe? Was it a shared account?

Hunter replies: "I promise be right down. Sorry."

Five minutes later, Rob texts Hunter again to say that Dale Pupillo, a retired Assistant Director of the Secret Service who used to guard his father, has arrived.

"He's going to front desk, call and tell them to give us a key now H," Rob texts.

"As your friend, we need to resolve this in the immediate.

"Call the front desk now H or I will have to assume you are in danger and we will have to make them give us the keys."

"Really Rob I am coming down right now," Hunter texts nine minutes later. "I really promise. Was in the bathroom buddy. Coming right this second."

Thirty seconds later Rob replies: "We're at your door. Open it."

What these apparent minders told Hunter next isn't recorded. We know Hunter stays up the rest of that night, logging into an encrypted government site, "secure.login.gov," a number of times until 4:04 a.m.

He also will pay for a first-class United flight to Washington, DC, leaving later that morning, for an impromptu trip to see his father.

At this stage, Joe has been out of office for almost eighteen months, so neither he nor Hunter is eligible for Secret Service protection. According to his memoir, *Beautiful Things*, Hunter ended his Secret Service protection in July 2014, halfway through his father's vice presidency.

But Joe has remained close to Pupillo, a wiry Midwesterner who ran his protection detail for most of his time in office and who once nominated Pope Benedict as the person he most admired.

Joe earned the veteran agent's undying loyalty when he and Jill flew on Air Force 2 to Merrillville, Indiana, on September 11, 2009, to attend the wake of Pupillo's father, John. After Pupillo left the service in 2015 he continued to work for the Biden family in a private capacity.

Emails on the laptop indicate a close relationship.

"You are both wonderful people," Pupillo writes to Hunter and wife, Kathleen Biden, in March 2012, telling the couple he has been transferred out of the vice president's detail.

"You have become a part of the family. Much love," replies Kathleen.

Another email from Pupillo relates to business dealings with the Bidens after he retired from the Secret Service in 2015.

With the subject line "Invoices for the Ho investigation," requesting payment for "the background work we did," the email is forwarded to Hunter by his uncle Jim Biden on April 2, 2018.

Attached are three overdue invoices totaling $7,500, for "due diligence investigation and social media investigation" on three of Hunter's business partners, Tony Bobulinski, James Gilliar, and Patrick Ho.

It won't be long after the Hollywood intervention before Joe's Secret Service connections are called upon again to rescue Hunter from a crisis. But next time the clean-up doesn't quite go to plan.

CHAPTER

The Prodigal Son

"Politics is not the family business. Service is."
—**Hunter Biden,** ***Beautiful Things,*** **2021**

Hunter is indignant. He's left his Gucci bomber jacket at one of his favorite strip joints in Washington, DC, and the "dancer" last seen wearing it has vanished.

He's into the first night of a visit to the family back east after his dad's Secret Service friends bailed him out in L.A., where he'd been fleeced by a Russian hooker. Joe hopes the visit will bring an end to his debauches. Hunter has other ideas.

"It's a $8,000 Gucci jacket your buddy borrowed," he texts Sylvia, the manager of Archibald's Gentlemen's Club, on May 29, 2018, in the first of a series of irate messages.

"First, sorry I didn't get back the other night. I gave your friend about $700 in cash and apple-paid another $500 to her—still a shit move, but

I promise I had better than good reason. However, I obviously intended to come back because I left a Gucci $8,500 leather bomber jacket that was given to me by Alessandro herself."

Alessandro Michele, creative director of Gucci, is a man, so Hunter is talking malarkey. Sylvia says the stripper has gone to Germany and isn't answering her phone. Hunter becomes accusatory as another week goes by with no news.

"Really, Sylvia you and she were best friends according to you and you can't get word from her in Germany?

"We three were in the same private 'room' together and she was wearing my jacket that you commented on when you saw her wearing it. You specifically told me the girl you had chosen to join us was a good friend."

Sylvia replies: "We were never in a private room together. We sat in one briefly while you tried to PayPal her money, both of you went downstairs. I never saw her or you again. If you gave her your jacket and then left the club how is it anyone else's fault but your own?"

Hunter does not text Sylvia again, but the dispute doesn't stop him spending thousands more at the seedy K Street establishment, just three blocks from the White House, before the year is out.

He is known as a generous tipper who sits in the VIP room and pays his bills with "credit cards that didn't have his name on it," according to the *New York Post*'s Page Six.

The main purpose of the hastily organized trip home is for his father to straighten Hunter out and get him earning again instead of frittering away his life in L.A.

To that end, Joe urges Hunter to meet with a key Biden donor, Jeff Cooper, who ran one of the largest asbestos-litigation firms in the country. The Illinois-based SimmonsCooper began filing multimillion-dollar lawsuits in Delaware in 2005 in association with Joe's late son Beau Biden's firm Bifferato, Gentilotti & Biden, when Joe was a US senator for Delaware and leader of the powerful Senate Judiciary Committee.

"Call. I'm with Jeff Cooper," Joe texts urgently on Hunter's last Friday in Wilmington, June 15, 2018.

An hour later, Joe texts Hunter a cell phone number: "Jeff. Asked for you. Wants to do some work with you. Love Dad."

Cooper always was a reliable backer of Hunter's business career. He had made a lot of money from the $30 billion asbestos compensation business, in large part thanks to Joe, who used his position on the Judiciary Committee to block asbestos litigation reform when a bill reached the Senate floor, as Paul Sperry from RealClearInvestigations has reported.

When Joe became vice president, Cooper put Hunter on the board of his venture capital firm Eudora Global and soon gave him shares in the business, which netted Hunter around $80,000 a year, documents on the laptop show.

Time and time again, Joe had used his connections to provide Hunter with prestigious and lucrative jobs, until he had a glittering résumé bulging with unearned privilege.

After Joe became vice president, Hunter landed a no-show role as "of counsel" for the New York–based law firm Boies Schiller Flexner LLP, a Democrat outfit associated with the Clintons. He wasn't obliged to keep office hours or attend meetings, but Boies paid Hunter $216,000 per annum, according to an email written on January 16, 2017, by his former business partner Eric Schwerin, then-president of Rosemont Seneca.

Schwerin also details in that email a windfall "one-time payment" of $300,000 two years earlier from Jeff Cooper's firm Eudora.

There also were earlier acts of generosity from SimmonsCooper, like the time the firm put up $1 million in investment capital for Hunter and Uncle Jim's abortive attempt in 2009 to run a hedge fund. It ended in tears, as did most of their ventures, and the Bidens had to give the money back.

With his father out of office, Hunter is restless and rootless on his short visit to Delaware in that balmy spring of 2018. He stays with Joe and Jill at their roomy lake house on Barley Mill Road.

There's no record of his contacting Cooper after missing the meeting with his dad. Instead, he texts strangers on Tinder and uses escort services such as "Sweetkink."

As recorded in raunchy photos on his laptop, Hunter reunites briefly with his sister-in-law turned lover, Hallie, in the waterfront house they rented in Annapolis, Maryland. He is obsessed with her in Byronic fashion, but, more than two years into their on-again, off-again relationship, she has tired of his deceits and jealousy.

Three days after arriving home, he already is withdrawing $1,000 a day from ATMs and texting his crack dealer: "Can you find something for me?"

His dealer delivers subpar product: "Man...I feel like the biggest sucker in Annapolis," Hunter gripes in a text.

The longer he stays, the more he is reminded of why he fled for L.A. in the first place. "Delaware is the worst place in the world for me," he confides to a friend. "Need to get away."

The relationship with Hallie is toxic. She is trying to get clean and is censorious about his drug abuse. He calls her a "stupid fucking cunt" and accuses her of cheating on him with a mutual friend, David, whom he stalks one night to a sports bar in Wilmington.

"You fucking pussy," he texts. "I'm sitting outside Rocco's, Dave. Come on out buddy."

Hallie has blocked Hunter from her phone, so he resorts to texting her thirteen-year-old daughter: "Natalie, tell your mom to call me. Not you. Thanks."

"Don't say anything hurtful," replies Natalie.

This gentle reproof sets Hunter off: "Natalie stay out of my business and never tell me what I can and cannot do. You're 13 and have no business telling me to shut up or anything in fact. And tell your mother I will not speak to her if you are in the room, house, car...now tell her damnit to call me now."

Hallie takes over Natalie's phone: "This is Hallie—If you need to discuss something with me, do it through your father as you told me to. Please do not tell Natalie to have me call you, she is too young."

It's the wisest thing anyone has said to Hunter in months.

He is ready to go home to the Chateau Marmont, where no one judges or shames. But even after he vanishes once more into his dissolute life in L.A., there will be unwelcome reminders of past transgressions back east reaching out to ensnare him.

"Just called to check in on you" comes the text on July 3, 2018.

It's from Lunden Alexis Roberts, a twenty-seven-year-old stripper who worked under the stage name "Dallas" at another Washington, DC, establishment, The Mpire Club.

There was a reason Hunter avoided The Mpire on his trip east.

Roberts is pregnant with his child, and he wants nothing to do with her or the baby.

Bender Ender at the Chateau

"A Crack-Heads Guide to Hotel Etiquette. OR Why Crack Cocaine is Better for You than Vodka but not as Fun as Crack and Vodka. OR Why Crack Cocaine and Air Travel are Easy: From The Delta Shuttle to Air Force One. (It's all good, brother, as long as you have a smoke buddy.)"
—Hunter Biden, titles for a book, Notes, June 2018

I
t takes a lot to get blacklisted from the Chateau Marmont, the HQ of Hollywood debauchery for ninety years. But in the summer of 2018, Hunter Biden manages to do just that.

Late at night, on Thursday, July 19, he is checking in at the front desk of the iconic Sunset Boulevard hotel, as he has done many times before. The night manager is about to hand over the familiar green silk–tasseled set of room keys when he notices a warning note on Hunter's file in the computer system. It stipulates the need to get preapproval from the general manager before booking him in.

"WTF man. Seriously WTF," Hunter rages in a series of indignant texts with Chateau bellhop Mike the following night.

"Seriously...a note in the system that says under no circumstances am I allowed in the building without her pre-approval. WTF man."

Mike replies: "That's fucked, let me text someone."

Hunter: "Fuck them. It was so fucking embarrassing. The two women at the desk were right there and said WTF."

Mike texts back a few minutes later: "Apparently you were banned for 'drug use' is what I was just told, which is bullshit."

Hunter: "Drug use???? You have to be fucking kidding me. I was banned for drug use at the Chateau Marmont. You have to be fucking me."

Mike: "Lol exactly. You don't have to tell me…. Let me talk to her tomorrow."

Hunter: "Well that's a fucking first in the Hotel's history I guess. Should I take it as a badge of honor? I really mean it, that literally must be a first at the Chateau. I have never ever been rude or have had a complaint against me from a guest or employee. I kind of thought I was an employee favorite. And they ban me without telling me directly. I have to find out from the night desk guy. Wow."

He keeps ranting at the bellhop about his banishment through the night, even after moving to another luxury hotel in West Hollywood, La Peer ("Cool hotel actually").

Later Mike texts again: "So I pulled up your profile. It does say 'BLACKLISTED.'"

Hunter: "How is that possible man. How could I have possibly been blacklisted. Is there a single person I have offended or been anything but obsequiously generous?"

Mike: "I know you are. I asked one of the reservation girls and she said there was a hole in the wall in one of the rooms you had."

Hunter: "A hole? Dude what does that even mean? And what does that have to do with drugs? And why would a hole in the wall not be something I paid to repair. And I've never put a hole in a fucking wall."

Mike: "Email the owner."

Hunter: "Ok. My dad getting here in a couple of hours."

It's not evident whether Hunter took Mike's advice and complained to the hotel's celebrity owner, André Balazs. But in his last recorded text exchange with Mike, in March 2019, Hunter whines that his family never treated his grudge against the hotel with the seriousness he felt it deserved: "I can be banned from the Chateau and told 'just leave it be.'"

A little over a year later, in the middle of the COVID-19 pandemic, most of the hotel's staff had been laid off, while Balazs was telling *Variety* he wanted to turn it into a private club for the uber-wealthy.

It was the end of an era for the "Castle on Sunset." The favorite haunt of hell-raising celebrities, from James Dean and Marilyn Monroe to Lindsay Lohan and Keanu Reeves, the Chateau had tolerated decades of bad behavior under the banner: "Always a safe haven."

Led Zeppelin rode their Harleys through the corridors, Scarlett Johansson and Benicio Del Toro reportedly hooked up in the elevator on Oscar night, Britney Spears had a breakdown in the dining room, and John Belushi died from a drug overdose, aged thirty-three, after a night of partying with fellow guests Robert De Niro and Robin Williams.

On its website, the hotel used to quote Columbia Pictures founder Harry Cohn: "If you must get into trouble, go to the Marmont."

At the time Hunter was blacklisted, guest shenanigans were spiraling out of control, according to the *Hollywood Reporter*. "Units were trashed at a rate never seen before." The thirteen-dollar-an-hour housekeepers had to contend with used sex toys left under beds and needles and bodily messes that required special biowaste containers.

But even the Chateau's Zen-like patience hadn't been able to withstand Hunter's 2018 mega-bender.

It was at the Chateau that spring where he learned to cook crack, using baking soda, acetone, water, and cocaine powder, which he would heat in a baby food jar in the tiny kitchen of his "garden cottage" by the pool, among the lemon trees and bougainvillea, where it was no surprise to find hotel guests snorting cocaine off their dinner plates.

Hunter's cottage became the honey pot for an "ant trail of [drug] dealers and their sidekicks [who] rolled in and out, day and night," he wrote in his memoir, *Beautiful Things*.

"They'd drink up the entire minibar, call room service for filet mignon and a bottle of Dom Perignon.

"One of the women even ordered an additional filet for her purse-sized dog…. [T]hey'd walk out with the hotel's monogrammed towels and throw pillows and comforters and ashtrays."

His new friends ripped him off too, racking up tens of thousands of dollars on his credit cards.

"Charges would roll in: Gucci loafers, an $800 sport coat, Rimowa luggage," he wrote. "I lost track of stolen wallets and credit cards…. I told family back in Delaware I was working on my sobriety—whatever the hell that meant at that point."

Hunter didn't mention in his memoir that he had been blacklisted by the Chateau, exactly. Instead, he claimed the hotel asked him to leave, quite unreasonably, because other guests complained about his visitors.

"I saw it as blatant racism and let them know it," he wrote. He doesn't explain why he made that assumption. We're left to conclude that the "ant trail" of hookers and drug dealers and hustlers he claimed had come to fleece him were mostly people of color—which seems, well, racist on his part.

Laying a racism charge against the hotel that had spurned him was a way to get a measure of revenge for Hunter, who kept harping on the insult for months.

After being turned away from the Chateau, Hunter settles into his new digs and texts a friend named Rush: "I'm at this really cool hotel called La Peer in West Hollywood… Come have a drink."

Rush replies: "I'm suuuuper stoned."

Hunter: "Ha. Cool. I'm here with a couple friends and my dad is stopping by later."

Joe Biden does fly in the next day to visit his son.

"Why is your dad here anyway? Just to hang w you?" his favorite cousin Caroline texts.

"He has something on in Phoenix and I'm sure here but he's saying it's just to see me," replies Hunter. "Whatever."

In fact, Hunter knows he is the reason his father has flown across the country.

He has been raging at Joe for over a week, accusing him of disloyalty in long, unhinged texts. He is convinced Joe is taking Hallie's side in their arguments.

Hunter's affair with his brother's widow had begun shortly after Beau's death in 2015, when he claims she "seduced" him.

He left his wife, Kathleen, and three daughters, aged fifteen, seventeen, and twenty-two, to live, off and on, with Hallie and his niece and nephew in her marital home in Delaware, two miles from Joe and Jill's lakefront spread. They moved in February 2018 to a $7,000-a-month waterfront home with a pool in Annapolis, Maryland.

But the couple's drug use was "out of control," according to Hunter's sister, Ashley.

After visiting them in early 2018, Ashley texted Hallie's sister Liz Secundy: "They are beyond messy! They left all their drug paraphernalia for my parents to see."

Hallie and Beau's marital home had become a party house where people would sit all night on the porch smoking crack.

Hunter also filmed many of his sex sessions with Hallie and would upload the videos onto his PornHub account for the world to see, with titles such as "Lonely Widow."

He paid $57,000 for her to go to rehab in Malibu in late 2017 but then railed against her efforts to get him to quit drugs. He was wildly jealous and accused her of sleeping with other men, projecting his own misbehavior onto her. They quarreled incessantly in texts and phone calls, some of which he recorded. He would search through her phone for evidence of infidelity when she was asleep and photograph unfamiliar numbers to google later.

Eventually, she said he couldn't see her children until he stopped using drugs and told him his father supported her edict.

"We clearly have two very different views of loyalty, Dad," Hunter texted Joe on July 11.

"You owe none to me if you are told by others without any evidence of it that if I'm using/drinking/whatever, people say you owe me no loyalty nor respect at all....

"Your vision of me being a hapless degenerate drunken crackhead is so unbelievably hurtful.

"I don't think we should talk for a while dad. I'm always amazed when you tell me you're on my side. 'It's all-out war, you're outraged, you won't allow her to do this to me, you're my son, of course I believe you.' And then you validate every single thing she has manipulated everyone into believing....

"You make a fool out of me...because she has already told everyone that you agree that the kids can't be with me unless you are present."

Joe tells Hunter he is wrong: "The question is where is your loyalty in believing a father who has never lied to you."

Hunter isn't buying it. "Just leave me alone for a while, dad, while I ponder my disloyalty to you."

Joe replies: "Your [*sic*] taking that out of context."

Hunter: "Oh ok then, sorry for what I said and sorry that she heard it the same way I did and has told everyone that you agree I shouldn't be alone with the kids.... Really sorry dad, but I'm finally done with all of it every bit of it."

The next day Joe texts to say he's coming to L.A. and adds an emotional plea: "I Need to hold you."

Hunter sends back a 555-word missive that reads in part: "Dad, if you want to come for you, come. If you are coming for me then I have to tell you I can't make you feel better and lie and say I understand Dad...I always want to make you feel better. I know you don't do anything to or for me that's not coming from a place of love."

He goes on to express his feelings of inadequacy and his lifelong yearning to be taken seriously by the father he adores.

"All that love can hurt a lot Dad. It can be used as a tool to get what you need. Which for twenty years has felt like you just needed me to go to my bedroom and be quiet while the grownups talk. You say you respect my opinion and my judgement 'BUT you're an alcoholic Hunter...I'm not sure I can run, Hunter, because of what it will do the family (i.e. I may not run Hunter because of all your fuck ups.)'….

"Unless you're coming to say 'I'm wrong and these are the reasons how I've been wrong' then believe me when I say I just don't have the energy right now to hear you tell me 'You took that out of context, Hunter. I never said that Hunter. You need to get healthy Hunter.' If that's all you have to give me Dad, more veiled criticism and advice… more excuses for why you are so justified because of the loss that you have experienced—the same exact losses I've experienced alongside you—then this will not go well."

Three days later Hunter belts out another furious text to Joe. "Dad did you go to Beau's today, kiss Hallie and hang out in the kitchen and talk to all of them, kiss Hallie goodbye, give her a big hug.… Once again as you can see from my knowing that…the way you act spreads like wildfire."

Joe replied: "Didn't kiss her, hugged [grandson] Hunter, asked if he could go to Janssens [gourmet market] with me ALONE. After breakfast dropped him off, did not leave driveway, her mother was leaving, started to rain, waived [sic] goodbye.…

"My word as a Biden on the health of my grandchildren…I am loyal and adore you.… She is trying to split you and me. I think she thinks I won't banish her because I'll loose [sic] my grandchildren. But…she will not succeed."

A few days later Hunter is sending long, angry texts to Hallie's daughter Natalie—just thirteen at the time—using her as a go-between in his escalating war with her mother.

"What do u want me to say to her from u?" asks Natalie.

"To stop lying and telling you she wants to speak to me.…Tell her that you want to meet whomever she has chosen to spend the life she decided a long time ago not to live with me.… She still will not let me see you without Pop [Joe] present—ask her why.… If it's driving I will never drive in a car with you again. Pop's coming to see me this weekend—ask her to send you too to come to my home in Malibu on the water."

Natalie replies: "OK I will but I don't [like] this, it gives me anxiety."

Hallie promptly forwards Hunter's texts to Joe and asks for his support. As a demonstration of paternal fealty, Joe forwards her text to Hunter. This is what she said: "Pop—This is inappropriate, hurtful, manipulative and wrong on so many levels. It's too much for Natalie. I am sober and having tests reported to you. If Hunt does not enter a program and get multiple tests weekly then I don't know how YOU could allow Natalie or Hunter anywhere near him…. I of course want him in the kids' lives, but his behavior is damaging them."

Joe flies to L.A. to do a welfare check on Hunter the day after he is evicted from the Chateau Marmont, although he is unaware of his son's dramas with the hotel.

Father and son have "an emotional morning" at La Peer, Hunter tells his friend, Azura.

"I'm taking him for a haircut. Sorry, we were engrossed. A very personal and long overdue talk."

Uncle Jim texts later that day to check the temperature: "How's it going with your dad? (1-10) 10 best."

Hunter: "7."

Jim: "Hang in there my friend. Rome wasn't built in a day!"

Joe leaves the next day, and Hunter moves to an Airbnb to resume his carousing.

"Should I come…I have mushroom pills," texts his buddy Rush.

"Yes please come," says Hunter.

"Wait, are you not staying at the Chateau anymore?" Rush asks in an earlier text.

Hunter doesn't tell him about the blacklisting: "I left just for a change of pace and a fear I would end up like that guy who wore the same all black outfit every day and creeped me the fuck out or the very nice guy with the little dog who…would talk to you for an hour about literally nothing."

It takes Hunter six weeks to pick up the belongings he'd stored at the Chateau. By that stage he is temporarily sober because Uncle Jim flew to L.A. to book him into an exclusive drug detox center in Brentwood. "The View" bills itself as a "luxurious six bed facility [with] pool, hot tub, patio, lush amenities, and breathtaking views...." with gourmet meals from an "on-site chef, massages, and yoga classes."

Jim tells Hunter he has wangled a discount for him: "Normally $4,000 a day per day for 10 days. Your deal $2,500 for 5 days guaranteed."

Afterward, Hunter is ensconced in a $1,100 a night Balinese-style Airbnb in the Hollywood Hills, but he resents having to share it with "my sober living companion 24/7."

He complains to Jim that the companion is a "complete moron" and an "idiot fat Jewish kid who insisted he had a right to enter the bathroom while I was on the toilet."

Hunter is in such a foul mood that even his long-suffering uncle is fed up with him: "Text/email your father your plans. I'm sick of getting kicked in the teeth. I'm out."

It's the only time Jim has ever complained.

But there was a far more precious relationship Hunter was pushing to breaking point.

Kathleen

*"Happy families are all alike; every unhappy
family is unhappy in its own way."*
—Leo Tolstoy, *Anna Karenina*

Kathleen Buhle was a sunny, pretty blonde from Chicago, with more than a passing resemblance to Hunter's late mother, Neilia. The daughter of a schoolteacher and a White Sox ticket salesman, Kathleen had just graduated from Saint Mary's University of Minnesota when she and Hunter met as volunteers at a Jesuit youth program in Portland, Oregon, in 1992.

Hunter had a BA from Georgetown University and was heading to law school. Ruggedly handsome, sporting a beard, a leather jacket, and a brooding demeanor, he wrote poetry and waxed lyrical about his favorite novel, *Post Office*, Charles Bukowski's tale of a down-and-out barfly.

They couldn't have been more different, and they fell head over heels in love.

He was assigned to help at a food bank in a church basement and, every afternoon, would catch a bus across town to see Kathleen, who was working in another church helping adults with disabilities.

Three months after they began dating, she unexpectedly fell pregnant. But within weeks they were throwing an engagement party at Joe and Jill's stately home in Greenville, Delaware, and were married in a Catholic church in Chicago, on July 2, 1993, Kathleen's slight frame just showing her four-month pregnancy.

She was welcomed by the Bidens at the start. Kathleen recalled in a speech at a charity event in 2013 that appears in draft form on Hunter's laptop: "Twenty years ago when I came into the Biden family, Pop [Joe] took me, nose to nose, and told me he loved me, and I was a daughter to him."

But it can't have been easy. In one of his anguished messages to Kathleen when their marriage was on the rocks two decades later, Hunter reminded her of how supportive he had been back then.

"Do you remember calling me to tell me you were pregnant? Do you remember me meeting you at the airport with books about pregnancy? 'What to Expect When you're Expecting.' Do you remember me being there every second, saying I loved you no matter what?"

A father at twenty-three, Hunter finished law school and soon grew bored with the lucrative executive role his dad had organized for him with his donors at MBNA insurance.

In 1998, Hunter moved his young family to DC for another six-figure salary in the Clinton Commerce Department, making a fat profit when he sold the historic home in Wilmington that he had bought two years earlier.

Two more daughters were born, Finnegan and Maisy. The girls would attend the elite Sidwell Friends school, where Maisy became best friends with Sasha Obama, the president's daughter.

Kathleen and the First Lady struck up a close friendship, too, sweating together at SoulCycle and Solidcore classes, dining with girlfriends on the back patio at Chez Billy Sud in Georgetown, having cocktails at the White House, even skiing at Aspen with their girls after the separation.

Kathleen also was friendly with her sister-in-law, a sultry brunette five years her junior. Hallie Olivere appeared on the scene after Beau took a job as a federal prosecutor in the US Attorney's Office in Philadelphia and moved into Hunter and Kathleen's big house. The daughter of a Delaware dry cleaner, Hallie had the same wild spirit as Hunter, whereas Kathleen and Beau shared a steady, conscientious temperament. It was as if the brothers had married the female version of one another.

In 2013, Kathleen described to *Washingtonian* magazine how she and Hallie enjoyed getting dressed together for inaugural balls: "We'll get our hair done, put our makeup on with all the kids running around."

Kathleen and Hunter were a good team socially, by all accounts. Friends described them in emails as "charming, interesting, fun."

"Kathleen is a devoted mother and a wonderful friend," Karen Barker Marcou told *People* magazine. "Her warm personality literally lights up every room she walks into."

In Washington, Hunter had moved into the capital's most lucrative industry, lobbying. But when Joe was chosen for his ticket, Barack Obama's advisers frowned upon his son influence peddling—and Hunter had to find another line of work.

Pop came to the rescue, calling on his stable of generous donors to find his son a soft landing. This time, with Uncle Jim Biden holding his hand, the hapless pair were tipped into ownership of a New York–based hedge fund, Paradigm Global Advisors, with a million-dollar investment from Jeff Cooper.

"Don't worry about investors," Jim Biden would say, according to an unnamed executive quoted by Politico. "We've got people all around the world who want to invest in Joe Biden."

The venture collapsed in acrimony and lawsuits, but by then Hunter was on to the next magic carpet ride.

He went into business with hunky ketchup heir Chris Heinz, the stepson of his father's colleague, Senator John Kerry, and Heinz's charismatic Yale roommate Devon Archer, a former Abercrombie & Fitch model. The genetically blessed trio set out to monetize their powerful family connections. On June 25, 2009, they founded investment firm Rosemont Seneca Partners.

Four years later Heinz will get cold feet and bail out of the partnership, but Hunter seems oblivious to the pitfalls of cashing in on his father's name in corrupt foreign jurisdictions.

He is "willing to take on risk," is how Archer puts it in an email to another partner, Bevan Cooney, now in jail. "Chris is much more risk averse. Hunter will work if we need him too [sic] as well."

"Work" for Hunter meant opening doors using his family name. In 2017, for instance, he boasted in an email about a three-year deal with one of his Chinese partners, CEFC chairman Ye Jianming, which guaranteed him $10 million annually "for introductions alone."

He does not appear to contribute anything in the way of strategic vision or corporate know-how to his various ventures, and seldom answers work-related emails. Much of his time, as recorded on the laptop, involves navigating his fraught personal life, feuding with family members, buying drugs, and organizing assignations with prostitutes.

But he also plays a crucial role, as a sort of gatekeeper, in his father's court, especially once Joe becomes vice president. Hunter is feted by a long line of people who come cap in hand to ask for favors from his father. Some want Joe to speak at a function or show up at a charity golf day. Others want him to swing an internship or a college place for their child.

Then there are those, such as associate judge John Mott, of the Superior Court of the District of Columbia, who are keen for a good word.

"Hi Hunter," Mott writes on March 8, 2010, in the first of several intense emails.

"I write to follow-up on our conversation at George and Karen's party and on Cristina's recent e-mail. My name is at the White House on a short list for the President's consideration for a vacancy on the United States District Court for the District of Columbia. The process has been a long one, with no decision made yet…. I would love to talk as soon as convenient for you. I am very grateful for your support…. It is great to have your help on this."

Emails also show Hunter writing directly to his father's various private email addresses to suggest people for roles in the administration.

"Before you fill position pls talk to me," Hunter wrote Joe on June 23, 2014, before suggesting a person named Johnny, who "very much wants to serve as detail fr [*sic*] treasury."

"Re Johnny call me right away. Dad," replies Joe.

Meanwhile, Kathleen, who describes herself in the divorce as a "stay at home mother," is busy ferrying the girls to sport, organizing potluck dinners with other families, shopping at Neiman Marcus, and contributing to charities for domestic violence survivors.

She and Hunter are featured regularly in the social pages. They are fixtures at White House State Dinners for foreign leaders. They rub shoulders with ambassadors, journalists, and members of Congress at embassy cocktail parties and DC book launches. They fly regularly on Air Force 2, whether for family weekends to Nantucket, ski holidays in Colorado, or treks to the Grand Canyon.

They are on *Washington Life*'s prestigious list of "notably social individuals" three years running.

In 2009 Hunter is named to the magazine's Power 100 as "Attorney and International Business Advisor: The Veep's son recently stepped down as Vice Chair of the Board of Amtrak in order to make his move in the Washington business community. Smart Move: The former corporate lobbyist changed careers in 2008 when his father ran for president; making him more difficult for Republicans to target."

Beau's death in 2015 shattered Hunter, but his drinking, drug abuse, and adultery meant the marriage was already in trouble before he fell apart.

The first public sign of tumult came when he was discharged from the Naval Reserve due to a positive drug test in 2013.

Joe had pulled strings to get Hunter a double waiver so he could follow Beau into uniform at the ripe old age of forty-two.

The first waiver was an exemption for his age. The second was to excuse an arrest for cocaine possession in 1988, when he was eighteen. Hunter had been placed on a pretrial intervention with six months' probation, and his arrest later was expunged from the record, he notes in his memoir. Ironically, that same year his father co-sponsored tough anti-drug legislation that strengthened prison sentences for drug possession and disproportionately punished African Americans.

Despite Joe's efforts, Hunter's naval career was over just a month after his father swore him in at a private ceremony at the White House on May 7, 2013. On the first day of his first weekend of Reserve duty, a random urine test detected cocaine in his system.

Hunter tried to fight his expulsion and came up with a farcical excuse. In a letter to the Navy, he suggested that he inadvertently had smoked cocaine-laced cigarettes that random strangers outside a bar had given him the night before he reported for duty, he told the *New Yorker*. He went so far as to brief a lawyer but ultimately decided against appealing the decision.

His official discharge came without fanfare the following February— an administrative rather than dishonorable discharge.

Hunter kept his shame to himself but prepared a draft statement on his laptop for the inevitable public disclosure: "After 10 years of sobriety I relapsed at possibly the most inopportune time. The guilt and shame I felt over letting myself and my family down was indescribable. I sought an age waiver at 42 years old to serve in the U.S. Navy. I dishonored that great privilege…and for that I am deeply ashamed. But I also know that I cannot allow one moment in time to define me."

The *Wall Street Journal* would break the story that October.

Joe forwards the story to Ashley, Beau, Hunter, and Kathleen: "Good as it could be. Time to Move on. Love Dad."

Kathleen replies: "I have never felt more love and support than I have today. The emails, phone calls and texts from so many, telling me they love us and know Hunt is a good man…. Everyone asking how they can help. This is the silver lining."

She and Hunter will begin couples therapy a few weeks later, which will continue through Beau's illness and death on May 30, 2015.

After Hunter delivers the eulogy at Beau's funeral to great acclaim, he confides to Kathleen on the drive home that he is contemplating a career in politics.

"Every third person I hugged or shook hands with encouraged me to move back to Delaware and run for office," he tells her.

Kathleen is aghast. "Are you serious?"

She reminds him he was just discharged from the Navy in disgrace. "So you really think you can run for Congress…don't ever say that to your children and embarrass yourself."

These are the words Hunter throws back in her face in an email months later. He is still griping about Kathleen's lack of faith in him in his 2021 memoir.

"We didn't say another word to each other for the rest of the ride. Or really, ever again."

CHAPTER

It's Over

"I was the sicko sleeping with his brother's wife."
—Hunter Biden, *Beautiful Things*, 2021

"I'm leaving you because you are having an affair and you have been emotionally abusive," Hunter's wife Kathleen emailed him in July 2016.

"I forgave you for cheating before, I tried to help you get sober and you made it clear, throughout the past year, that you didn't want to be with me. You didn't didn't want my forgiveness and you didn't want my help with your recovery.

"I cannot control how you will twist what has happened over the past year—how you will try to make it my fault—which seems as cruel as the cheating."

That is indeed what Hunter did to Kathleen, his wife of twenty-two years, when he told the world his version of the disintegration of their marriage in his 2021 memoir.

By his account, it was Kathleen's failure to forgive him at his hour of greatest need, right after Beau's death of brain cancer in 2015, that triggered his spiral into drugs and adultery. Finally, she drove him into the arms of Beau's widow, Hallie, the only woman who understood his pain.

"I was fortunate to have Hallie's support after Beau's death and when I was estranged from Kathleen. Our world had been completely upended, and we turned to each other for strength and solace," writes Hunter in a draft media statement on his laptop, July 30, 2017, three months after his divorce.

"I regret the loss of my marriage…. But my relationship with Hallie had nothing to do with Kathleen asking me to move out of our home two months after Beau died." Hunter is adamant that he and his sister-in-law didn't become a couple until fourteen months after Beau's death.

But Kathleen would come to believe the affair began within days of the funeral. At first he made her feel "crazy" for doubting him. Hunter swore blind that his long absences from their family home in the fashionable Tenleytown neighborhood of northwest Washington, DC, were because he was needed back in Wilmington to comfort his brother's grieving widow and two children, ten-year-old Natalie, and nine-year-old "little Hunter."

Hunter dismissed her growing unease about the situation and characterized any complaints about the time he was devoting to Hallie as callous. He stoked feelings of inadequacy and guilt in a way that only someone who knew intimately her trusting and kindly nature was able to do.

Three weeks after Beau's death, with Hunter spending all his time in Delaware with Hallie and her kids, Kathleen confides in her husband about her misery and confusion.

"I don't think I can fully explain why I'm upset," she writes to Hunter on June 21, 2015, after visiting him at Hallie's house. "I just know I've been sad since you came to Delaware.

"I think it's watching you with Hal and her kids. It made me sad to hear you all playing and laughing in the bedroom, sad to have Hal tell me what a really great family moment it was, how nice it was to watch TV with you. It made me sad to hear you casually say you'd go with Hal to take Natalie to camp....

"You being the good guy through this and me being the sullen one, with you constantly looking at me like you don't understand why I'm upset, just exacerbates everything."

"I'm sorry you feel that way," Hunter coolly replies. "I thought we talked about me staying over to pick out the headstone for Beau tomorrow morning with Dad."

He goes on to provide an elaborate explanation of his movements the previous evening in Hallie's house, where he says he slept on a "Murphy bed in the den."

"I laid down with Hunter in his room—then I joined Finnegan and Hallie and watched part of a movie we all have seen...then I took my iPad and sat alone in the garage and watched a show."

Six weeks after Beau's death, and three days after their twenty-second wedding anniversary, Hunter has moved out of home.

That Friday, July 3, 2015, Hunter had stormed out of a couples' therapy session and downed a bottle of vodka. He caught an Uber to Archibald's strip club, near the White House, and did not return home until 5:00 a.m., receipts show.

The next night, Hunter was with Hallie, who had been invited by vice president Joe to drive down from Delaware with her children to celebrate Independence Day.

"Pop [Joe] called and asked if we would go to DC for the 4th," Hallie had texted Hunter. "We could watch fireworks from White House or Nana's [Jill's] office."

Joe had suggested he could take little Hunter and Natalie with him to Vancouver on Air Force 2 to watch the United States play Japan in soccer's Women's World Cup the next day.

Hunter, who was planning to be at home in DC that weekend, urged Hallie to come: "I have to be in Delaware early Monday so I could drive you back Sunday afternoon."

On July 4, Hunter ordered an Uber from his house in Tenleytown to the nearby VP's residence, arriving just in time for the 9:07 p.m. fireworks.

But something happened that weekend that finally made Kathleen's doubts crystalize. It was "because of his conduct" on the night of July 4, Kathleen would later tell a divorce court, that she asked Hunter to leave.

Hallie's children were staying overnight with Joe and Jill before heading to Vancouver on Air Force 2 for the World Cup Sunday, along with Hunter's daughter, Maisy, then fifteen, and her friend, Sasha Obama.

Hunter appears to have driven Hallie the two hours back to Delaware to the empty house she once shared with Beau. His diary records that he was still in Delaware on Monday July 6, with one item listed in his diary—an 11:00 a.m. "corporate finance call" with Burnham Asset Management, the ill-fated firm that would see his partner Devon Archer facing jail on fraud charges five years later.

He emails his marriage therapist at 11:40 a.m. to say he won't make it back in time for his appointment.

He is due back in DC Tuesday, for a meeting scheduled with his father and three of Joe's closest political advisers, Steve Ricchetti, Mike Donilon, and Ted Kaufman, at the vice presidential residence. Joe is preparing to announce a run for the White House.

Kathleen still holds out hope of saving their marriage, but she is insisting that Hunter go to drug rehab before he comes home.

"Hunter, I think about you all day," she writes him on July 28, 2015. "I feel physically sick because I don't feel like I am helping you…. I hope we can come up with a plan…. I love you Hunter and hope at some level you feel that love."

Hunter replies in a tone that is more conciliatory than it has been in months: "It's very simple to me. I love you—you love me—we love our girls—we love our family. I need you now. You need me now…. I need my best friend. You need your best friend…. I am broken and flawed but no one loves you more than me."

Days later, *New York Times* columnist Maureen Dowd, described by Hunter as his father's favorite journalist, writes that Joe is seriously considering a run at the White House, under the headline: "Joe Biden in 2016: What Would Beau Do?"

"The 72-year-old vice president has been having meetings at his Washington residence to explore the idea of taking on Hillary [Clinton] in Iowa and New Hampshire….

"But going through the crucible of the loss of his oldest son, Beau, to brain cancer made the vice president consider the quest again."

Dowd wrote that Beau "had a mission" before he died. "He tried to make his father promise to run, arguing that the White House should not revert to the Clintons and that the country would be better off with Biden values."

A few months later Politico would report that Joe himself was the source of the leak to Dowd and had effectively "placed an ad in the *New York Times*" to launch his campaign, a suggestion Joe angrily denied, although he later confirmed Dowd's tale in his memoir, *Promise Me, Dad*.

"The idea that I would use my son's death to political advantage was sickening," Joe would write. "I was afraid I would not be able to control my rage."

Throughout the summer of 2015, Joe tests the water for his candidacy, but enthusiasm is lukewarm, with the media according Hillary Clinton advantages on the grounds of age, gender, party support, money, and campaign infrastructure. She is unbeatable, in other words.

Kathleen emails Hunter from their lake house in Indiana, where she and their youngest, Maisy, sixteen, have retreated for the summer to be with her parents.

"Do not mention again how long ago Beau died. I have no one to turn to with all of this so, trust me, I know how long I've felt alone…. You and I haven't talked in over a month except for one time where you yelled. One email is good, the next makes me feel like I've been punched.

"You are not ok. My gut is you have been using this entire time…. You are still projecting on me, denying what is really going on and so far as I can see, not working on sustained sobriety."

On August 24, Breitbart breaks a story that Hunter's name and credit card details have been found on a hacked cache of user data from the website Ashley Madison, a dating service for married people that uses the slogan "Life is short. Have an affair."

Hunter denies using the service and claims he has been hacked by Russians. Blaming the Russians is a tactic that Hunter and his father will use again, four years later, when his abandoned laptop threatens to derail Joe's run for the 2020 presidential election.

"EXCLUSIVE! Joe Biden's Son: Ashley Madison Account Was Created In My Name By America's Enemies," ran the Breitbart headline.

"Hunter Biden tells Breitbart News that the account is not his, but rather was created by one of America's enemies to discredit him. He thinks it could have been due to his sitting on the board of a Ukrainian gas company, which outraged supporters of Vladimir Putin's Russian regime."

Hunter insists to Breitbart that he is not the "Robert Biden" listed as a client of Ashley Madison, even though he confirms the email address listed on the account belongs to him and the date of birth is the correct day and month, though ten years younger.

"I am certain that the account in question is not mine," he is quoted as saying. "This is unfortunately not the first time that someone has used my name and identity to try to discredit me."

Behind the scenes, a flurry of emails between Hunter and his business partner Eric Schwerin shows them trying to spin the response to Breitbart.

"I do strongly feel that there should be some line in the statement that basically says, 'fuck you' I'm a private citizen and you are scumbags," Hunter writes in exasperation.

"I know," replies Schwerin, "but I think it is too confrontational and we just want this to be a one-day story and done."

The *Daily Mail* has other ideas. The day after the Breitbart story appears, Hunter receives an email from Francesca Chambers, the *Mail*'s White House correspondent.

"Mr. Biden, I've seen your statement on the Ashley Madison incident, but several questions remain unanswered based on the file we saw....

"Chief among the unanswered questions: whether the credit card used to set up and pay for the Ashley Madison account was yours. If not, why was a credit card with your name on it registered to an address linked to you...and used to pay for $268.99 in services on Ashley Madison on 06-25-2014?

"Do you believe yourself to be the victim of criminal-level identity theft?"

Hunter does not respond.

Kathleen is humiliated by the story. But a few days later Hunter tells her it's her fault that people think he's a cheat and a liar: "I have struggled with this disease. And when I need you most to protect me against myself you shut me out....

"My brother died and the day after he was put in a grave you stopped speaking to me.... Your absence after the most devastating moment in my life clearly confirmed to all our friends and family that I truly must be the most despicable human being in the world....

"Everyone already thinks I'm a lying cheating piece of shit. My mother and my sister-in law and everyone in my family, they all hate me because what you have told them. The only response I get is 'you deserve it.'"

Kathleen: "I'm trying to get to a place where I can trust you again and I don't know how.... I have this unsettling feeling that you are keeping things from me."

Hunter: "I've consented to daily breathalyzers and blood tests and urinalysis and meetings with psychologists and still from afar you influence the process. You say I'm angry. I'm not angry. I'm amazed and disappointed.

"The person I fell in love with and have always been in love with is now my enemy.... Have I ever missed a tuition payment or mortgage payment, a play or a game or anything that ever mattered—or your Neiman Marcus bill.

"Do you know what I've done to make that possible? Do you have any idea of the level of degradation?"

The degradation he has to endure to keep the money rolling in seems to be very much on his mind.

Within days of his angry email to Kathleen, Hunter attends a State Department luncheon Joe is hosting for the visiting Chinese president, Xi Jinping, whose patronage Hunter enjoys by proxy.

"All international politics is only personal," Joe tells Xi and assembled guests, including Henry Kissinger. "If you can't establish a personal relationship where you understand one another, it's awfully hard to get anything done. And more than four years ago, President Obama and... President Hu decided that then-Vice President Xi and I should get to know one another."

It was a relationship that would prove spectacularly profitable for the Biden family.

At this stage, in September 2015, speculation about Joe's presidential ambitions has reached a crescendo.

NBC News quotes anonymous sources saying Jill Biden "is fully behind" the vice president for his third run at the White House.

The *Boston Globe* runs a story that Joe has invited Massachusetts senator Elizabeth Warren for lunch at the Naval Observatory to float the idea of being his running mate. "If I have my way, you'll be living here," he reportedly tells her.

On October 11, Hunter tells his therapist he needs to spend time in Delaware, away from his wife and children because he is having important meetings there with his father and his father's close friend "Sen. [Ted] Kaufman and others about the possible Presidential race.... I have to go to begin a vetting process."

The next day Kathleen writes to Hunter offering to delay the divorce "until after your dad decides or campaign ends. I don't want to impact that it any way. I hope he runs. Maybe that will be a good distraction for you."

She also tells him he is "a better father than your dad…I know you love your dad and I do too but he wasn't perfect…. You were better, in every way."

By October 21, 2015, it's all over. Joe announces he won't run for president, referencing Beau's death in an emotional statement in the Rose Garden, flanked by Jill and President Obama.

"As my family and I have worked through the grieving process, I've said all along…that it may very well be that that process, by the time we get through it, closes the window on mounting a realistic campaign for president. I've concluded it has closed."

The following month, Hunter is complaining to his new divorce lawyer that Kathleen is "making life miserable. She is draining the bank accounts—and telling her family and my girls that I am withholding money from her. She has now created a scenario by which my relationship with Hallie started long ago and that I've disgraced the family….

"She has gained access to my emails and my texts. I could care less if it wasn't such a strange violation of privacy and sharing her version of the last few years with kids to vilify me just makes me so sad."

Yes, Kathleen's worst suspicions about her sister-in-law and her husband have been confirmed. Any hopes she might have had of saving her marriage were dashed after she found steamy texts between Hunter and Hallie on an old iPad.

"That gave her the gift of justification," Hunter wrote in his memoir. "I was the sicko sleeping with his brother's wife."

"You say you were surprised by my asking for a separation," Kathleen writes to Hunter in her email of July 2016.

"I was surprised when I found your bottles of Viagra and Cialis [erection enhancing drugs].

"I was surprised when I found airline purchases and jewelry purchases…. Not only did you cheat on me…you actually bought her expensive gifts….

"It has taken a long time for me to process that the man I loved, the marriage that I thought I would be in for the rest of my life, is gone.

"I've been able to really reflect on how you've treated me and realize the emotional abuse you have subjected me to over the past year. Your taunts about Beau, Natalie and Hunter. Your telling me that I'm crazy.... Your denials of the cheating and what now appears to be an affair....

"I hope you can stop lying about everything and forgive yourself for what you've done. I've forgiven you—I just won't take it anymore."

After twenty-one years and three beautiful daughters it was a brutal end to their marriage.

Kathleen filed for divorce on December 9, 2016, asking for sole custody of sixteen-year-old Maisy.

Then things got ugly, fast.

On January 11, 2017, in an email to a friend, Hunter complains that while he was on the phone with Kathleen that night she had told their daughters: "Dad and Aunt Hallie were FUCKING the day after Uncle Beau died."

He accuses his friend of taking Kathleen's side: "I don't know what story you've been fed that would lead you to conclude I am a pathological liar.... It really really was devastating to me that you adopted Kathleen's narrative....

"I remember Kathleen saying, 'if you mention little Hunter crying for his dad every night one more time I'm going to puke.' I remember her saying that it was 'ridiculous how much the entire family was focused on Hallie and her kids.' She said that a month after Beau died."

Kathleen emails Hunter asking him to settle the divorce "quickly and kindly to respect the marriage and family we had....

"I am beyond frustrated with your alternative facts regarding our finances. Simply looking at your spending is enough for any judge to be disgusted....

"I have tried everything. Contractual separation, mediation, using the same lawyer, everything.... I don't want to hear about how you two pay the bills. I don't care about your business. I just want a fair settlement so I can plan my future and finances."

On February 17, 2017, Kathleen's lawyer Rebekah Sullivan writes to Hunter's lawyer Sarah Mancinelli: "Hunter is in possession of a large and extremely valuable diamond. Please provide proof that the diamond has been placed in a safety deposit box…by noon tomorrow or we will have no choice but to ask the court, on an emergency basis, to enjoin his further dissipation of assets, including the diamond."

Mancinelli replies: "There is no diamond in Hunter's possession."

Behind the scenes, she asks Hunter for more information. "I don't know what else to tell them," she writes. "If you can craft a couple of sentences for me to send her I would appreciate it."

But there really was a diamond—a glistening 3.16-carat specimen worth an estimated $80,000, which Hunter had been gifted earlier that month in Miami by the shadowy chairman of Chinese energy conglomerate CEFC, Ye Jianming. The handsome thirty-nine-year-old tycoon with the patronage of President Xi and links to the People's Liberation Army was Hunter's highest-ranking and most generous business partner in China to date.

By this stage, Kathleen's checks to the housekeeper have bounced three times, and bills are piling up to medical providers and therapists. The credit cards are maxed out, and more than $300,000 in unpaid taxes hang over their heads.

"Your spending is documented and irresponsible," Kathleen writes Hunter on February 20, 2017.

"I am sick of trying to figure out how you are hiding the money."

Three days later she files a new motion in the DC Superior Court accusing Hunter of "spending extravagantly on his own interests (incl. drugs, alcohol, prostitutes, strip clubs and gifts for women with whom he has sexual relations), while leaving the family with no funds to pay legitimate bills.…

"His spending rarely relates to legitimate family expenses but focuses on his own travel (at times multiple hotel rooms on the same night), gifts for other women, alcohol, strip clubs, or other personal indulgences."

She tells the court Hunter has blown through $122,000 in two months and had reduced payments to her and their daughters from $17,000 a month to just $1,700.

Hunter denies hiring prostitutes or going to strip joints. But straight after Kathleen's bombshell allegations hit the news, he chooses to go "directly to a strip club. I said, 'f--k them,'" he tells the *New Yorker*.

A few days later, Page Six breaks the news that Hunter and Hallie are an item: "Beau Biden's widow having affair with his married brother."

Hunter has convinced Joe to give his blessing to the union: "We are all lucky that Hunter and Hallie found each other as they were putting their lives together again after such sadness," the VP tells Page Six. "They have mine and Jill's full and complete support and we are happy for them."

On April 14, 2017, the day she is granted a divorce, Kathleen, forty-eight, sobs in court. Hunter is not there. He is living in Delaware with Hallie.

But the $37,000 alimony he will have to pay her each month, at a time when much of his income has dried up as a result of Joe leaving office, will put a strain on his finances that will lead him to take more and more risks for cash and only further fuel his crack addiction.

CHAPTER

The Delaware Way

*"I hope you all can do what I did and pay for everything for this
entire family for 30 years. It's really hard. But don't worry, unlike Pop, I won't make you give me half your salary."*
—Hunter Biden, text message to daughter Naomi, 2019

I t was a simple plan Joe devised for his sons.

Beau was the golden-haired prodigy who would go into politics
as the next JFK, remaining squeaky clean and above reproach on
his road to the White House. He would move from federal prosecutor
to Delaware's attorney general, en route to the governorship and perhaps
the Senate.

Hunter, who would have preferred to be an artist or a writer, was
assigned the role of paying the bills for the rest of the family through
lucrative grace-and-favor jobs and sweetheart deals facilitated by Joe's
network of connections in Delaware and, later, throughout the world.

To understand the Biden family's international influence-peddling operation, you have to know where it all began, in the chummy political culture of the small state of Delaware.

For more than four decades as the senator for Delaware, Joe had leveraged a quid pro quo system of cronyism and trading favors for political influence, which has come to be known as the "Delaware Way."

He and his associates have spun it as a cordial system of bipartisanship where everyone comes out a winner.

But federal prosecutors investigating corrupt campaign donations involving the Bidens described the Delaware Way more accurately as "a form of soft corruption, intersecting business and political interests, which has existed in this State for years."

In that case, wealthy Delaware liquor distributor Chris Tigani, forty-one, whose father had played football with Joe at Archmere Academy, took a plea in 2011 and was sentenced to two years' jail. The court was read an email Tigani sent to the president of Anheuser-Busch boasting that he was "the number one fundraiser" for Joe and would play a role in his 2008 presidential bid and in Beau's political career. "They are very good and close friends and I know that we can take advantage of that relationship as needed."

Beau Biden was Delaware attorney general at the time and recused himself from the case because he, also, had received campaign contributions from Tigani.

Tigani wore a wire for the FBI and recorded people close to the Bidens. But nothing ever touched Joe or his family.

The acting Delaware US attorney overseeing the case at the time was David Weiss—the same David Weiss who is the U.S. attorney in charge of an investigation into Hunter Biden, launched in 2018, over alleged tax violations, money laundering, and Chinese business associations.

According to Politico, the investigation into Hunter had reached a point in the summer of 2020 where prosecutors "could have sought search warrants and issued a flurry of grand jury subpoenas."

But Weiss was advised to pause the probe, "to avoid taking any actions that could alert the public to the existence of the case in the middle of a presidential election." It is not reported who delivered the advice, and the inaction is presented as a virtue, but its effect was to protect Joe's campaign from the consequences of his family's venality.

"To his credit, he listened," a person involved in the lobbying of Weiss told Politico in July 2021.

By the time he became vice president, Joe had mastered crony politics in his home state. Soon he would extend the "Delaware Way" template internationally, by using Hunter, under the guidance of Joe's devoted younger brother Jim Biden, as bagman for the family.

Hunter effortlessly absorbed the lessons of Delaware from his father, though with slightly less finesse. At one point, when a Chinese business partner questioned his profligate spending, he snapped off an angry email: "If you refuse to sign the wire Kevin…. I will bring suit in the Chancery Court in Delaware—which as you know is my home state and I am privileged to have worked with and know every judge on the Chancery Court."

Over thirty-six years as a senator, Joe had become expert at not getting caught doing anything illegal or too obviously unethical. Never be too greedy, never leave a trail, never say too much—and always, but always, play the sympathy card if the heat comes on.

Still, it came to rankle with Hunter that he was viewed as the family's cash cow, while never receiving the credit he thought he was owed for his financial contribution.

"Beau didn't take on these fucking responsibilities. He didn't do any of this shit. I swear to fucking Christ he didn't," he raved to a friend in Los Angeles one drunken night caught on voice memo in 2018.

"I love all of you. But I don't receive any respect," he wrote the following year in an email to his oldest daughter Naomi, then twenty-five.

"I hope you all can do what I did and pay for everything for this entire family for 30 years. It's really hard. But don't worry, unlike Pop [Joe], I won't make you give me half your salary."

Of course, every inflated salary Hunter was paid, every board appointment, every lobbying client, and every lucky break he owed to Joe.

There wasn't much on his life's résumé he could claim as his own. Little wonder that he would grow insecure and resentful.

Joe had his heart set on Hunter attending Yale, the most prestigious, most selective law school in the country, where GPA and LSAT scores in the 99th percentile are prerequisites for automatic admission.

Although his prep school grades from Delaware's Archmere Academy have never come to light, Hunter was better known for drug scores than academic scores in his youth.

But it was 1993, and a Democrat was in the White House.

Daniel Golden, author of *The Price of Admission: How America's Ruling Class Buys Its Way into Elite Colleges,* takes up the story in a 2019 article for the *Chronicle of Higher Education*: "Guido Calabresi, then dean of Yale Law School, received a call from the White House. Yale Law's most powerful alumnus, President Bill Clinton, asked him to let in a Georgetown University graduate named Hunter Biden, according to two people familiar with the incident. Hunter was the younger son of Joe Biden, then chair of the Senate Judiciary Committee....

"Calabresi, who had walled off the dean's office from the admissions process at Yale Law to avoid just such pressure, told Clinton that he would not intercede. The admissions office then rejected Hunter."

Having failed to meet Yale's admission standards, Hunter had to content himself with Georgetown. But the following year, he quietly scored a transfer to Yale.

What had changed?

Golden claims Calabresi kindly met with Hunter after his rejection and suggested an alternative path to entry: attend another law school, then reapply to Yale as a transfer student.

"Hunter took his advice. After a year at Georgetown's law school, Hunter was admitted to Yale in the summer of 1994, soon after Calabresi stepped down as dean."

Calabresi subsequently was nominated by President Clinton to become a judge on the US Court of Appeals.

He sailed through the confirmation hearing after his nomination was put forward by none other than Senate Judiciary Committee Chairman

Joe Biden, "with the recommendation that [it] be confirmed," notes the *Congressional Record* of July 15, 1994.

There is no evidence that Calabresi directly intervened in Hunter's admission to Yale or any suggestion that he was not well qualified for the role. He was following in the footsteps of one of his predecessors as dean, Louis Pollak, who went on to become a judge on the US District Court.

But just three years before Calabresi's elevation to the bench, Joe had presided over a far more brutal confirmation hearing, that of Clarence Thomas, which the first African American Supreme Court justice famously denounced as "a high-tech lynching for uppity blacks who in any way deign to think for themselves, to do for themselves, to have different ideas."

In his memoir, Hunter maintains that his admission to Yale had nothing to do with family influence. Instead, it was the rare quality of a poem he submitted that made him stand out from the crowd: "Yale's acceptance letter noted that my success and dedication...more than qualified me but that my poem was unlike anything they'd ever received." Hunter claims his score on the generalized law school admission test was only slightly under Yale's median: "Guess that 172 on my LSAT counted for something."

However it was that he finally was admitted to Yale on his second attempt, Hunter's magic carpet ride delivered him to student lodgings in New Haven, with wife, Kathleen, and baby Naomi in tow.

He graduated in 1996 and returned home to Wilmington in time to work as deputy campaign manager for Joe's Senate reelection campaign.

Joe then wielded his clout with campaign donors to place his son in a series of high-paying jobs. Fresh out of college, aged twenty-six, Hunter made more money than Joe, whose salary as a US senator at that time was $133,600 per annum.

It was expected that Hunter would use his outsize earnings to pay off his own student loans as well as Beau's.

He was still harping on the tuition burden twenty years later in an email to his aunt, Valerie Owens, Joe's younger sister, and the surrogate mother who had moved in to help raise him and Beau after their mother died.

"Dad co-signed each loan then which was only $7,500 per semester which we both took in loans in our names," he wrote. "I was a third year at Yale and had already secured a job that would pay all [Beau's] tuition…. Dad never paid one dime."

Hunter often griped that he was forced to give half his salary to his father. There's no direct evidence of such a wealth transfer to Joe on his laptop.

But we do know that Hunter routinely was paying at least some of Joe's household bills, including his monthly AT&T bill of around $190.

We know from an email with the title "JRB bills" to Hunter from his business partner Eric Schwerin on June 5, 2010, that Hunter was expected to foot hefty bills to Wilmington contractors for maintenance and upkeep of his father's palatial lakefront property. Joe's initials are JRB, for Joseph Robinette Biden.

The bills that month included $2,600 to contractor Earle Downing for a "stone retaining wall" at Joe's Greenville estate, $1,475 to painter Ronald Peacock to paint the "back wall and columns" of the house, $1,239 to builder Mike Christopher for repairs to the air conditioning at the cottage of Joe's mother, "Mom-Mom," which was on his property.

"This is from last summer I think and needs to be paid pretty soon," wrote Schwerin of Christopher's bill.

Another $475 "for shutters" was owed to RBI Construction, of Bear, Delaware, about fifteen minutes west of Wilmington.

Schwerin's email to Hunter begins: "FYI, there are a few outstanding bills that need to be paid and I am not sure which ones are a priority and which should get paid out of 'my' account and which should be put on hold or paid out of the 'Wilmington Trust Social Security Check Account.'"

He goes on to explain that "there is about $2,000 extra in 'my' account beyond what is used for monthly expenses." It is unknown why Schwerin used quotation marks around "my." In any case, it appears the account is used to pay monthly expenses for the Biden family.

Three days later Schwerin writes Hunter again: "Mike Christopher [builder] is hassling me so I am paying a couple of the smaller things since I haven't heard from your Dad. Know he's busy—so it's OK. But if you think he has a moment or two to review the email I sent you let me know."

In another email to Hunter on July 6, 2010, titled "JRB Future memo," about a plan apparently devised for Joe's future wealth opportunities, Schwerin writes: "Does it make sense to see if your Dad has some time in the next couple of weeks while you are in DC to talk about it? Your Dad just called me about his mortgage…so it dawned on me to might be a good time [for] some positive news about his future earnings potential."

Other documents on the laptop suggest a mingling of Joe's finances with Hunter's.

In an email on April 12, 2018, to his assistant Katie Dodge, Hunter complains that he has been "shut out" of one his Wells Fargo bank accounts.

"Too many cooks in the kitchen. Too many profile changes and such. Happened 10 days ago too…. My dad has been using most lines on this account which I've through the gracious offerings of Eric have paid for past 11 years."

Further evidence that Joe expected to receive a slice of his son's income was provided by Tony Bobulinski, Hunter's former business partner in a firm named Oneida, which was set up to enter a joint venture with the Chinese energy conglomerate CEFC. Bobulinski says that Joe was the "big guy" referred to in a 2017 email who was to be allocated 10 percent equity in the firm: "10 [percent] held by H [Hunter] for the big guy."

Perhaps it was black humor, but in 2014, when Hunter was enmeshed in dubious moneymaking schemes in at least five countries where Joe wielded power, Schwerin emailed him a quote from the then-VP, answering a question about "the professional choices made by his children" that aired on WLWT in Cincinnati.

"I should have one Republican kid who'd grow up to make money," Joe said.

Joe helped out his son financially in less direct ways, through his business connections in Delaware, the nation's corporate tax haven. "American Liechtenstein" it was named in the Financial Secrecy Index, which crowned Delaware the world's most opaque jurisdiction, attracting capital from around the world, with no questions asked, and where legislation beneficial to financial services interests is worked out with lawmakers behind closed doors.

Aged just twenty-nine, and a small-time Wilmington councilman, Joe won his US Senate seat in 1972 in a narrow upset over Republican two-term incumbent Caleb Boggs, sixty-three, on a platform of generational change and opposition to "politics as usual."

According to a book about mob hitman Frank "The Irishman" Sheeran, president of Teamsters Local 326 in Wilmington, Joe owed his win to a union-organized newspaper strike before the election, which stopped a Boggs campaign ad from reaching voters.

"This maneuver is what got Senator Joe Biden elected," Sheeran claimed in the 2004 deathbed biography, *I Heard You Paint Houses*— whose macabre title is a mob euphemism for the mess a hitman makes when he blows someone's brains out. Martin Scorsese's movie *The Irishman* was based on the book.

"Republicans say that if those newspaper inserts from the Boggs' side got delivered inside the newspapers it would have made Joe Biden look very bad."

Joe, who had never worked a union job, thereafter became a Teamsters man, said Sheeran. "You could reach out for him, and he would listen."

The hitman also claimed to have murdered Teamsters boss Jimmy Hoffa. After Hoffa's unsolved 1975 disappearance, the Bidens remained close to his family.

"Senator Biden has always been a friend to working families and is a key Teamster ally," said Teamsters General President Jim Hoffa, Jimmy's son, when endorsing Joe for vice president in 2008, despite the senator's history of supporting trade policy that disadvantaged American workers.

Hunter invited Jim Hoffa to a state dinner at the White House for Germany's Angela Merkel in June 2011. Also in attendance that night was

John Brennan, then-Homeland Security Advisor, and his wife, Katherine, regular fixtures at fancy White House events in the Obama years.

Contemporaneous reports from November 1972 show that there was indeed a strike of the Printers Union, that Teamsters truck drivers refused to cross a picket line, and that the newspapers with Boggs' ad were not delivered.

It's hard to know if it made a difference to the election, but in the end Joe only won by 3,000 votes. He has dominated this most peculiar state ever since, in ways only a handful of insiders will ever fully understand.

And so it happened that, in 1997, a newly married Hunter lucked into a rare real estate goldmine, buying a historic house set in the lushly landscaped 1,000-acre grounds of the Winterthur estate of Henry Francis du Pont, regarded as the loveliest of the two dozen Du Pont estates dotted through the bucolic countryside about six miles north of Wilmington.

Winterthur "seemed like a European duchy, a private Ruritanian fiefdom carved out of America through the power of great wealth spent without stint," *American Heritage* magazine gushed.

The stone-fronted, four-bedroom house Hunter bought had been a "servant cottage" and was just a 500-yard stroll through the gardens to the 175-room Du Pont mansion turned museum.

Beau, then a federal prosecutor in Philadelphia, moved in with Hunter and Kathleen, while Hunter paid the mortgage and household expenses, he told the *New Yorker* in 2019.

The following year Hunter sold the house for "roughly twice what he'd paid for it," he told the magazine. In his memoir, he claims it was the hard work he and his family put in on weekends restoring the house that accounted for the price delta. "We scraped, caulked, primed and repainted every square inch of the place."

Like his father, early on Hunter evidenced an uncanny knack for making money from Delaware real estate.

A five-minute drive south of Hunter's place, down the Brandywine Valley Scenic Parkway, past the Wilmington Country Club, in the exclusive enclave of Greenville, Joe had bought a Du Pont mansion of his own in 1975, when he was a thirty-two-year-old recently widowed senator on a salary of $44,600 per year.

The grand 10,000-square-foot five-bedroom estate, with pool house, basketball court, and manicured gardens, was "the kind of place a thousand Italian guys died building—hand-carved doorways, a curving hand-carved grand staircase that Clark Gable could have carried a girl down, a library fit for a Carnegie, or Bernard Baruch, someone like that," wrote Richard Ben Cramer in his 1988 book on presidential candidates, *What It Takes*.

This was the mansion where Hunter and Beau—and their half-sister Ashley, eleven years younger than Hunter—grew up and learned to appreciate the finer things in life, among the country clubs and sumptuous estates of Delaware's "Chateau Country."

Joe paid $185,000 for the two-acre property he dubbed "the Station." He sold it twenty-one years later, in 1996, for $1.2 million, in circumstances that would later attract controversy. The buyer of Joe's house was John Cochran, the vice-chairman of MBNA, the Delaware credit card giant that would give Hunter his first job.

Journalist Byron York looked into the house sale for the *American Spectator* after it was raised as an issue in Joe's 1996 reelection campaign.

Joe's Republican opponent was suggesting what a lot of people were whispering, that Cochran had paid more than twice what the house was worth in a corrupt "sweetheart" deal.

Joe slammed the allegation as "the underbelly of politics, immoral and unethical," and gave his local Wilmington paper, the *News Journal*, a written appraisal of his house that fixed its value at exactly the price Cochran paid, $1.2 million. A second appraisal provided by Cochran put the house value at the identical price.

Joe claimed his "considerable renovations" of the mansion accounted for its steep rise in value.

However, York found that the place still needed quite a bit of work before Cochran could move in: "contractors and their trucks descended on the house for months after the purchase."

In addition, York found that the second appraiser had compared Joe's home to three other nearby houses that, in every case, had sold for about 20 percent below their appraised value.

When Cochran moved into the house, MBNA reimbursed him $330,115 for expenses related to the move, even though he was only moving from Maryland, no more than 100 miles away. A statement filed with the Securities and Exchange Commission stated that $210,000 of the expenses were to compensate Cochran for a loss on the sale of his Maryland home—an amount that worked out to roughly 20 percent of the purchase price.

"It appears that MBNA indirectly helped Cochran buy the Biden house," York concluded.

Joe's next property purchase was equally canny: a secluded waterfront just two miles from his old place, on which he built his palatial three-story dream home.

The acquisition of four acres on the shores of Little Mill Creek Lake in 1996 "involved wealthy businessmen and campaign supporters, some of them bankers with an interest in legislation before the Senate, who bought his old house for top dollar, sold him four acres at cost and lent him $500,000 to build his new home," the *New York Times* reported in 2008, while finding no evidence that Joe "bent any rules."

Nevertheless, Joe's Midas touch had struck again.

He bought the land from controversial real estate developer—and campaign donor—Keith Stoltz for $350,000, the same price Stoltz had paid five years earlier, according to the *Times*. Stephen Pyle, an artist who moved to Texas, had sold the land to Stoltz in 1991 and expressed surprise that the developer, who lived on a neighboring estate, did not make a profit selling to Joe. "That doesn't sound like Keith Stoltz," Pyle told the *Wilmington News Journal*.

The *News Journal* also reported that Stoltz owned a company that had proposed a controversial $525-million development project at nearby Barley Mill Plaza. The project ultimately was bogged down with lawsuits from wealthy residents until Stoltz gave up and sold the land a decade later.

To build his house, Joe took out a construction mortgage of $400,000 with the local Beneficial National Bank whose executives were "active in state politics in Delaware, major campaign contributors to both parties nationally" reported the *Times*. The bank's executives also advocated bankruptcy reforms that disadvantaged consumers, reforms Joe supported in his powerful role as head of the Senate Judiciary Committee.

Joe contracted builder Chuck Lattif, a friend of his brother Jim, to construct the sort of custom luxury house he specialized in creating for the blue bloods of Bryn Mawr, Pennsylvania, forty miles northeast.

It took twelve months to build Joe's sun-drenched Georgian-style pile on the lake's edge, facing due south across the water to a peaceful vista of wooded groves and rolling hills. Joe added a swimming pool, underground garage, and private jetty. It was here that he ran his presidential campaign during the 2020 COVID-19 pandemic, from his famous "basement," in reality a wood-paneled study installed by custom craftsmen. Honking geese from the lake outside Joe's window often interrupted interviews.

Twenty-five years after Joe bought his patch of Delaware paradise, Zillow estimated the compound to be worth nearly $2.9 million.

Joe liked to describe himself as the "poorest man in Congress." But he lived like a king, and the sorts of things that ordinary people save for and fret about for their family were never a concern.

Hunter's role was to be the conduit to cash that sometimes was short for those who lived lives of service but still required luxury. This was the family business.

Most law school graduates take years to work their way up to junior partner, but straight out of college in 1996, Hunter landed a $100,000 job, plus undisclosed signing bonus, with MBNA, his father's single largest donor.

He soon became a senior vice president and reportedly was nicknamed "Senator MBNA" by colleagues for his clout in Washington, where Joe championed legislation favorable to his firm in the Senate. For instance, Joe supported reforms that made it harder for consumers to declare bankruptcy and write off credit-card debt, and he helped kill off stronger protections for people "forced into bankruptcy who have large medical debts or are in the military," according to the *New York Times*. Wenli Li, an economist at the Federal Reserve Bank of Philadelphia, would blame the loss of bankruptcy protections for the sharp rise in home defaults and foreclosures that led to the financial crisis of 2008.

When the Obama campaign was vetting Joe for the VP spot on their ticket, his connection with MBNA was "one of the most sensitive issues" they examined, the *Times* reported in 2008.

That year NBC's Tom Brokaw asked Joe about "your son being hired right out of law school by a big company here in Delaware that's in the credit card business, MBNA. He got about $100,000 a year, as I recall. You received $214,000 in campaign contributions from the company and from its employees.

"At the same time, you were fighting for a bankruptcy bill that MBNA really wanted to get passed through the Senate making it much tougher for everyone to file bankruptcy....

"In retrospect, wasn't it inappropriate for someone like you in the middle of all this to have your son collecting money from the big credit card company while you were on the floor protecting its interests?"

"Absolutely not," said Joe, in a brazen defense of Hunter he has perfected over the years.

"My son graduated from Yale Law School. The starting salary on Wall Street is $140,000 a year as a lawyer, options he had. He came home to work for a bank, surprise, surprise."

Joe's figure of $140,000 is a stretch. The median starting salary in 1996 for the top law school graduates at the largest New York firms was $85,000, according to the National Association for Law Placement.

In any case, Hunter left MBNA in 1998 for his next grace and favor job in the Clinton Commerce Department, and the company continued to pay him a $100,000 annual retainer as a lobbyist for five years.

His father's longtime campaign manager and lawyer William Oldaker called in a favor from then-Commerce Secretary William Daley to get Hunter his next job. Three years later, when the Bush administration took over, Oldaker took Hunter under his wing in Washington at the lobbying shop Oldaker, Biden & Belair.

Hunter was able to burnish his résumé with corporate board positions, including with Eudora Global, an investment firm founded by one of his father's biggest donors, Jeff Cooper.

Prestigious directorships at nonprofits followed. Joe's powerful Democrat ally, Senator Harry Reid, reportedly helped out with an unpaid gig for Hunter on the board of Amtrak, whose taxpayer subsidies Joe always has backed.

"Hunter Biden has spent a lot of time on Amtrak trains" was how Democratic Senator Tom Carper of Delaware described Hunter's qualifications at his nomination hearing.

In 2011, Hunter was named chairman of World Food Program USA, the American fundraising arm of the United Nations–related nonprofit. Described by the *Wall Street Journal* as an "unpaid board of the politically connected," WFP USA would become a useful pretext for him to meet foreign oligarchs, ostensibly to solicit donations, even though the charity's fundraising role was purely domestic. Like Amtrak, it relied heavily on taxpayer largesse.

For Hunter, doors glided open and opportunities landed at his feet, even as his marriage fell apart.

Washington had taken to heart the well-worn axiom Joe's staff used to recite during his Senate years: "Joe says that when someone helps his family, it's just like helping Joe," Sam Waltz, a Wilmington business consultant who covered Joe as a young reporter, told *The Nation*.

By his own admission, Hunter had traded on his family name all his life, but it wasn't until his father became vice president in 2009 that the riches really started flowing.

Millions of dollars sloshed through the crude influence-peddling scheme he and Uncle Jim had devised with Joe as their silent partner. Hunter was living like a prince in pre-revolutionary France, chomping on $500 Oro Blanco cigars from Davidoff on Madison Avenue, scooping up $30,000 Brunello Cucinelli outfits from Riflessi on Billionaires Row.

He flew around the world on private jets and Air Force 2, partied in Monte Carlo, Lake Como, Acapulco, and Shanghai with foreign oligarchs in their ill-gotten mansions, and gorged himself on crack cocaine with an endless parade of beautiful Eastern European prostitutes.

It would be his father's cultivation of China's future president Xi Jinping that would provide his family's most lucrative payday. The joint venture agreement with CEFC was worth millions, and it specified a 10 percent share for his father, "the Big Guy."

But it also would bring Hunter to the brink of ruin.

CHAPTER

Oedipus Wrecks

"I am Damos...anger personified."
—Hunter Biden poem, January 2019

Even Joe Biden's most ardent supporters conceded that his performance against Donald Trump in the 2020 presidential debates was feeble, but one moment won him wide acclaim.

Goaded by the president about his crack addict son, he dismissed Trump's questions about Hunter's shady business dealings and looked straight into the camera as if he were speaking directly to the American people: "My son, like a lot of people, like a lot of people you know at home, had a drug problem. He's overtaken it. He's fixed it. He's worked on it. And I'm proud of him."

It was a masterful jujitsu countermove. He turned an attack on Hunter's venality into an opportunity to showcase both his boundless fatherly devotion and his moral outrage at the brute, Trump. He made a now-familiar call for sympathy, but this time he inserted his private sorrow into a bigger tragedy engulfing the country.

With an opioid epidemic ravaging working-class America, scorning drug users as criminals and degenerates had fallen out of favor. Though earlier in his career Joe had backed legislation that put more black and poor addicts behind bars, by the fall of 2020 he had come around fully to the enlightened view. Addiction was not a moral failure but a disease. To treat it otherwise was to afflict the sufferer with one of the most debilitating psychological effects of his condition—shame.

And shame was something Joe Biden knew well.

To understand the pathology that would see a loving father expose his drug-addicted son to the irresistible temptations of gushing torrents of unaccountable cash, you have to go back to Joe's childhood.

His early life might have been lifted out of a short story by John O'Hara, the chronicler of family tragedies, steeped in drink and disappointed ambition, in the Pennsylvania coal country.

Joe's father, Joseph Biden Sr., by all accounts was a dreamer and teller of tall tales. Tall, dark, and dashingly handsome, Joe Sr. was the son of a long-serving district manager of the American Oil Company in Scranton. After school he took a job with the company as a clerk/typist before moving into sales. Aged twenty-five, he married Jean Finnegan, a strong-willed second-generation Irish-Catholic Scrantonite, on May 30, 1941.

Joey was born the following November, followed by Valerie three years later, Jim in 1949, and Frank in 1953.

One of the few photographs of Joe as a baby shows his parents and maternal grandparents posing together on a wintry Scranton street, the picture of grim Irish respectability. The only person who looks as if he's having a good time is dapper Joe Sr., and that may be on account of the highball he's clutching in his left hand.

When Joey was two, his father left the oil company and moved the family to Boston for a well-paid job in his uncle's booming wartime business, Sheen Armor Company, which made sealant for merchant marine ships. But within two years, Joe Sr. had decided to go into business for himself, with a series of ill-fated ventures: a furniture store, an airport, and a crop-dusting service in Long Island, New York.

As an adult, Senator Joseph Robinette Biden Jr. would romanticize his father's early life, remembering him as if he were a character out of *The Philadelphia Story*. "My dad grew up well polished by gentlemanly pursuits. He would ride to the hounds, drive fast, fly airplanes. He knew good clothes, fine horses, the newest dance steps," Joe boasted in his 2008 memoir *Promises to Keep*.

But by the time Joey was six, the family was broke and had to move in with Jean's parents in Scranton. Joey would spend the next four years crowded into the Finnegans' modest gray clapboard on North Washington Street, with his parents, siblings, grandparents, his aunt Gertie and uncle Edward. Eventually his father found a job selling used cars, and the family moved to Wilmington.

Joe would blame the abrupt decline in family fortunes on the changing business climate at the end of the war, but other factors must have been at play.

He would never drink alcohol and explained in a rare moment of candor on the campaign trail in 2008: "There are enough alcoholics in my family." Joe denied that his father was a drunkard, but his niece Caroline said otherwise. In a text to Hunter, she described their grandfather as an "old school 1930s alcoholic."

That would explain the deep insecurities that helped form Joe. A boy with a stutter who was bullied at school and carried deficiencies of spelling and punctuation into adulthood, young Joey developed into a Walter Mitty–like character with a compulsion to be someone other than who he was.

By his own account, he overcame the stutter by standing for hours in front of a mirror reciting the speeches of his idol, the first Irish-Catholic president, John F. Kennedy, and dreamed of following in his footsteps.

Joe was put on a pedestal by the rest of the family. "As it did with the Irish kings, primogeniture rules," a 1981 *Esquire* profile said, "and Joe, being the oldest, gets, as his brother Jimmy puts it, 'the first helping, the biggest slice of the pie.' On that, Jimmy adds, raising his right hand, you can have his 'word as a Biden,' which is something the Bidens say when they're really telling the truth."

Within the family, loyalty was paramount. "Blood of my blood," they would say. "Bone of my bone."

Marty Londergan, who grew up with Joe, told *Esquire* about the neighborhood game of two-hand touch they would play on weekends against a team from one of the DuPont plants.

"Every weekend there would be a fight, with Joe Biden right in the middle of it, usually up against someone half again his size. It was, says Marty, his 'fast mouth.' Finally, the games stopped. No one wanted to play with Joe anymore. As Marty puts it: 'The guy just wanted to win too much.'"

Belying an easygoing, aw-shucks demeanor was a burning self-belief and drive for respect that would propel him, improbably, to the White House on his third attempt at the age of seventy-seven.

Along the way, he had his teeth burnished to ultra-white brilliance, covered his premature baldness with hair plugs, and disguised fits of ill temper with an instant thousand-watt smile that charmed and repelled equally. Named one of the ten best-dressed men in the Senate, he was described in 1974 by Kitty Kelley in a profile for the *Washingtonian* as looking like "Robert Redford's Great Gatsby in natty pin-striped suits, elegant silk ties, and black tasseled loafers. He dresses rich."

Appearances were always important to Joe Biden Jr., and he would work hard to cultivate a wholesome *Leave It to Beaver* image for his extended family. Privately, he aspired to the wealthy Kennedy clan's Camelot dream, from annual family holidays to Nantucket—the snobbier sister island to the Kennedy haunt, Martha's Vineyard—to the sprawling Biden compound in Greenville, where relatives and advisers would plan presidential runs.

He constructed a mythical persona full of tall tales of derring-do, exaggerations, and outright lies about his accomplishments. He lied about nonexistent academic awards and scholarships. He plagiarized speeches willy-nilly, and in one infamous case, appropriated the personal life story of British Labour Party leader Neil Kinnock, pretending that he, too, was descended from coal miners and was the first in his family to get a college degree "in a thousand generations."

He routinely repeated far-fetched stories with himself as the big guy, including a favorite in which he single-handedly faced down a "bad dude" named "Corn Pop" who was armed with a straight razor and "ran a bunch of bad boys."

He pretended that he trained as a racial activist in black churches, claimed he was at the center of the civil rights movement in Selma and Birmingham, and stated he had been arrested in Soweto on his way to see Nelson Mandela in prison. None of it was true.

Each lie served to boost his ego, to place him as the shining superhero of every grandiose story, smarter, tougher, more honorable than anyone, with the best marriage, the best children, the best house, the best life.

Even when caught out, he repeated the false tales. He seemed to have no shame, as if he had come to believe his own fantasies and had some psychogenic compulsion to share them.

His rubbery relationship with the truth extended to the powerful family mythology he created around "Being a Biden," with an emphasis on loyalty, omerta, and looking good. The only time his confabulations tripped him up was when he brazenly appropriated Kinnock's proletarian origin story, a scandal that forced him out of his 1988 presidential run.

And if ever he felt his idealized self-image was challenged, he would fly into what can best be described as controlled narcissistic rage.

This inner weirdness is captured in a video of Joe at a campaign stop in New Hampshire in 1987, angrily berating a man who asked politely what law school he went to and how well he did.

"I think I probably have a much higher IQ than you do," said Joe, jabbing the air with his finger and crisply enunciating each word. "I went to law school on a full academic scholarship, the only one in my class who had a full academic scholarship, and...ended up in the top half of my class.... I was the outstanding student in the political science department at the end of my year. I graduated with three degrees from undergraduate school.... And I'd be delighted to sit back and compare my IQ to yours."

He flashed a wide grin at the end that softened an outburst, which, even had his claims been true, was a wild overreaction, as the startled faces in the room attested.

Of course, his claims were false, as the newspapers reported at the time: there was no "full academic scholarship," his grades were poor through college in Delaware, and he finished near the bottom of his class at Syracuse Law School—seventy-sixth of eighty-five.

He also was almost expelled in his first year for plagiarism. He did not win an award for outstanding political science student, and he graduated with one degree, not three.

It is an illuminating moment, offering a rare glimpse into Joe's tightly wound inner self and a hint of the conflicts that must come from being his son. Seeing Joe explode on the campaign trail at impertinent questions, as he did a few times in the early stages of his 2020 presidential run, before the pandemic locked him in his basement, is a hint of the darkness within. You imagine a little boy when that finger starts thrusting and the shouting begins—and there is no mother to protect him.

Despite his powerful position over sixteen years on the Senate Judiciary Committee, which he chaired for eight years, Joe's fabulism made him a figure of fun in politics, albeit a lovable one. He had been taken under the wing of sympathetic older Senate colleagues when he first arrived and been fast-tracked into plum positions. But he soon developed a reputation in Washington as a "smart ass," said *Esquire*, with "the attention span of a gnat."

"All kidding aside" became a favorite line. Nobody serious took him terribly seriously, but they accepted the self-narrative of a humble, well-meaning family man, a conspicuous Catholic whose foibles were harmless.

Moreover, sympathy for the genuine tragedies afflicting Joe gave him a Teflon shield to override the misgivings people usually have about pathological dissemblers—or even the native distrust voters generally have for politicians. When a man has lost his wife and baby daughter in a car crash and his two little boys lie injured in hospital, no heart can remain closed.

But even in the context of this immense tragedy, Joe lied.

On the cold blustery afternoon of December 18, 1972, a truck carrying corncobs T-boned the white Chevrolet station wagon Neilia Biden had steered through a stop sign at the intersection of Valley and Limestone Roads in Hockessin, Delaware, on her way home from picking up a Christmas tree with her three children.

Neilia, thirty, and thirteen-month-old Naomi in the front seat, were killed. In the back seat, three-year-old Beau suffered a broken leg and two-year-old Hunter had head injuries.

The police file went missing, as did the hospital records, but by all contemporaneous news accounts, the crash was a tragic accident. No charges were laid. There was no suggestion of alcohol being involved.

The driver of the truck had right of way and appeared to have done everything humanly possible to avoid hitting Neilia's car, including over-turning his rig while swerving to avoid a collision.

And yet, almost thirty years later, Joe had rewritten the story in his own mind and shifted the blame onto the innocent truck driver, Curtis Dunn—but only after he died.

"It was an errant driver who stopped to drink instead of drive and hit—a tractor-trailer—hit my children and my wife and killed them," he said in a 2001 speech at the University of Delaware, two years after Dunn's death.

Joe embellished the false story over the years.

In an article titled "How Grief Became Joe Biden's 'Superpower,'" Politico reported that, while campaigning in Iowa in 2007, Joe told a crowd, "A tractor-trailer, a guy who allegedly—and I never pursued it—drank his lunch instead of eating his lunch, broadsided my family and killed my wife instantly and killed my daughter instantly and hospitalized my two sons."

He only stopped spreading the fabrication after Dunn's distraught family told reporters it wasn't true, and he was forced to apologize.

Nevertheless, the tragedy of the bereft widowed father had become an essential element of his identity, embodied by the iconic black and white photographs of his official swearing-in as a US senator at the hospital bedside of his injured sons, which were central to his campaigns from that day forward.

The pathos was captured early on by Kelley in her profile "Death and the All-American Boy" in *Washingtonian*, published eighteen months after the car crash.

"Some detractors accuse him of shrouding himself in widower's weeds, of dredging up his late wife in every speech," Kelley writes.

"In his office in the New Senate Office Building surrounded by more than 35 pictures of his late wife, Biden launched into a three-hour reminiscence. It wasn't maudlin—he seemed to enjoy remembering aloud. He was the handsome football hero. She was the beautiful homecoming queen. Their marriage was perfect. Their children were beautiful. And they almost lived happily ever after.

"Neilia was my very best friend, my greatest ally, my sensuous lover. The longer we lived together the more we enjoyed everything from sex to sports. Most guys don't really know what I lost because they never knew what I had. Our marriage was sensational. It was exceptional, and now that I look around at my friends and my colleagues, I know more than ever how phenomenal it really was....

"She had the best body of any woman I ever saw. She looks better than a Playboy bunny, doesn't she?" he says, showing Kelley a photograph of his late wife in a bikini.

It is a revelatory interview, in which Joe revels in the power of his new position. "Whether you like it or not, young lady," he says to Kelley at one point, thrusting his finger at her, "us cruddy politicians can take away that First Amendment of yours if we want to."

Joe also peppers his conversation with self-aggrandizing references to the Kennedys, who still loomed large over American politics six years after Robert Kennedy's assassination.

"Rose Kennedy is always calling me to come to dinner," said Joe of JFK's mother. "She has invited me at least ten times and I've only gone once. Most guys would kill to get invitations like that, but I don't accept them because I like to be with my children as much as possible...."

"Whenever Ted and Joan Kennedy call me for dinner—and they call quite a bit—I usually say I have to go home."

Forging a career in the Senate often meant long nights away from home for Joe. His devoted twenty-nine-year-old sister, Val, and her then-husband, Bruce, moved into his house in Wilmington after the crash to take care of little Beau and Hunter, with the help of Joe's mother, Jean, who Hunter dubbed "Mom Mom."

Various other members of Joe's extended family pitched in, including his brother Jim, who briefly opened a nightclub instead of going to college and whose street smarts Hunter admired.

Growing up, Hunter felt like he and Beau were "communal property," he told the *New Yorker*. "Everyone had a hand in raising us."

As an adult, Hunter called his aunt Val "my mother" and the person "I love the most." When he spoke of the late Neilia, he called her "Mommy."

Joe married twenty-eight-year-old divorcée Jill Jacobs in 1977, when Hunter was seven. The schoolteacher daughter of a Philadelphia banker, Jill was noted in Wilmington for wearing a full-length fur out to dinner at a local pizza joint, *Esquire* reported.

Hunter's beloved aunt Val moved out of the house when Jill moved in, and the boys had to readjust to a new family setup. Hunter called his stepmother "Mom," although the relationship was fraught at times.

Jill Biden did her best, left in a big house to manage two motherless boys, under the watchful eyes of her new in-laws. But for Hunter, emotionally abandoned by a father pursuing a big Washington career and abruptly separated from the aunt and grandmother he adored, a stepmother could never fill the void.

"When Beau was alive, he completely balanced out the lack of approval from my mother, the lack of love from her, but now there is no balance and I've come to believe her judgment of me, my mother's judgment of me, more often than not," he wrote to Hallie's sister Liz, four years after Beau's death.

"I made my mom [Jill] the center of my ego, the one whose judgment and approval I needed most.... Like every good addict I seek out what is most painful and difficult, like the relationship I have with my mom, and I mirror that relationship in the women I choose to love because I continue to have and hold onto the false belief that I can fix it, that I can make them love me."

In his self-pity Hunter later would complain that Jill preferred to play golf than be present for him in his childhood.

He and Beau thought Joe "walked on water," he wrote in his memoir, while hinting at some awkwardness with Jill. He felt left out when Jill joked with Beau, "sometimes directing their humor at me…. I was more sensitive or maybe just less mature and was as often confused by their jokes as I was in on them.

"My new mom was doing a great job, especially with everyone watching. Although she showed her deep love for me in ways I only fully understood later…the rhythms and dynamic of our new home were now slightly different. I was confused by that. I started to act out in school, not in alarming ways just small silly rebellions."

He ran away from home once and, from his hiding place in a tree in the garden, heard Beau "telling our mum between sobs that she was the reason I took off."

Hunter felt Jill loved him less than she did the sunny, straightforward Beau, as he told therapist after therapist.

Even his relationship with his beloved older brother is marked by ambivalence. Beau was everything Hunter was not. Hunter was the Goofus to Beau's Gallant, as one observer put it. Beau always knew the right thing to do, whereas Hunter was fretful and impulsive, getting into scrapes that his big brother would rescue him from with a hug. Hunter learned to get along by adopting an Eddie Haskell–style smarminess around adults.

"Beau and I were, by all accounts, the two unique halves of a whole," Hunter wrote in an unpublished statement in 2017 to counter speculation about his affair with Hallie. "We never had a cross word. We never did anything but love and adore and respect and honor one another. We never saw our accomplishments or our failures as apart from one another."

But Hunter's insecurity about growing up in an admired brother's shadow emerges in texts and emails to friends and acquaintances. He carps again and again about being under-appreciated.

To Hallie's sister Liz, he complains about having been treated like "an absurd and incompetent fool who only exists in the world of the deserving through his brother's accomplishments."

Hallie and her friends used to call him "Johnny Drama behind my back," referring to a pathetic character from the TV series *Entourage*. Hunter was deeply wounded by the slight and harped on it regularly, as the affair with Hallie grew increasingly tempestuous.

He described himself as "the loser brother always following along behind his superstar brother picking up the crumbs he left on the floor. [Hallie] told me that she and Beau would laugh about my stupid antics behind my back. That my brother didn't really think as highly of me as I thought he did. And once (exact words) 'Well you were always disappointing him.'"

Hunter's resentment toward his family spilled over in the last days of Joe's vice presidency in 2017, when he wrote his father an angry letter, accusing him of lying that Jill "saved this family" when thanks was owed instead to Joe's sister Val.

He was provoked by the "proudest moment" of his dad's vice presidency, a ceremony in which President Barack Obama presented Joe with the Presidential Medal of Freedom, an honor that had been bestowed on Pope John Paul II and President Ronald Reagan.

Joe wept when he received the medal in front of family and friends in the State Dining Room of the White House on January 12, 2017.

In a long speech, he described how much he had leaned on Hunter, "who continues to, in a bizarre kind of way, raise me.... Mr. President, you observed early on that when either one of my boys would walk in the room, they'd walk up and say, 'Dad, what can I get you? Dad, what do you need?'.... We've never figured out who the father is in this family."

Joe then paid tribute to his wife: "Jill came along, and she saved our life.... She gave me the most precious gift, the love of my life, the life of my love, my daughter, Ashley."

Hunter brooded over the speech for two days before firing off a 750-word screed to his father: "Dad, you have to listen—then you can do whatever you want.... You can ignore it or I hope at least acknowledge that the three people on earth who have lived their lives in service to you…have suddenly all concluded for their own reasons that you have finally crossed the line—that we won't be publicly and privately humiliated while those that publicly and privately humiliate us are held to the world as the loves of your life.…

"Love is an action, dad, not an emotion. Think how your brother and sister express their love for you. They do anything you tell them to do and have their whole lives.… Uncle Jimmy is my best friend and aunt Val is my mother—and if you make me ever feel like saying that is somehow a betrayal then know this: every time over the last 30 years you say 'She saved OUR lives' with aunt Val standing right next [to you] and never mention her I feel like grabbing the mic and saying she [Jill] may have saved HIS life but Beau and I were pretty happy with Mom Mom [grandmother Jean] and Aunt Val.

"Losing Mommy [Neilia] was more like I expect it might be to be born without legs—you know something really really important isn't there but don't quite know why it feels so incredibly absent when you can't remember its presence. And then you learn to walk and get bionic legs and a set of wings. Mom Mom and Aunt Val saved MY life Dad, they saved Beau's life, Dad.

"I understand the lie serves your purpose, Dad, but to make two boys who had the three greatest mothers god could conceive taken from them [feel] that they had to buy into it or they would be betraying you is pretty awful."

The next day, Hunter is still steaming when he writes a poisonous missive to his half-sister Ashley: "First I call the Kreins [Ashley's husband Howard's family] and let them know, yes, you're an addict." It gets much worse.

Ashley doesn't return fire. In future messages she will remain loving and patient toward the brother she idolizes.

Hunter's ambivalent attitude toward his father also emerges in conversations with his therapist Keith Ablow, who also variously acts as friend, landlord, and potential collaborator in a book or podcast.

The pair joke about Joe Biden's "dementia" in text messages in 2019.

On January 2, when they are discussing candidates in the Democratic presidential primary, Ablow declares: "Your dad is the answer," and then adds a mock endorsement: "'Any man who can triumph over dementia is a giant. Think what he could do for our nation's needed recovery.' Dr Keith Ablow."

Hunter replies: "You're such an asshole but that made me laugh out loud."

Ablow, still quoting himself: "'Perhaps he can help us remember all we intended to be as a people since he can now remember his address.'"

Hunter replies: "He doesn't need to [know] where he lives Keith that's the only thing the secret service get right at least 75% of the time."

In a separate text exchange on February 6, 2019, about a planned podcast, Hunter texts: "Dad is our first guest."

Ablow replies: "Perfect. Does he recall details tho, with the dementia and all."

Hunter: "Not much these days but since it's all fake news anyway I don't see the problem."

Reached at his Massachusetts office, Ablow declined to comment, but he once diagnosed then-Vice President Biden as having "early onset dementia" during a 2012 appearance on Fox News, so that background may underpin the banter.

Hunter often acted as the go-between for a line of people wanting favors from Joe, and there were signs that the role was wearing thin.

For instance, on March 18, 2017, Beau's friend Rob Buccini forwarded an invitation to Hunter for an event for the "Conservation Fund in Delaware" and asked if he could pass it on to his father.

Hunter replies: "Just tell me when, where, how much etc. As for my dad, fucking ask him yourself. Oops—did that just potentially end our relationship? Never mind, I will of course ask my dad to come and do "ME" a favor so he can hold it over me as he does every little chit or chat that's ever been."

As Joe's career approached its apogee, and the goal that had eluded him twice before was finally within his grasp, Hunter's resentment grew dangerously ungovernable, until he seemed to be sitting on a volcano of rage.

He liked to make rambling audio recordings of himself while he was driving, sometimes clearly stoned or drunk. In two such recordings in early 2019, soon before he abandons the laptop, he refers to his parents and himself in a spoken poem. He free associates, sounding a bit like Allen Ginsberg playing the Acropolis.

"I am Damos, son of Aries and Athena, Aries the hated god of war, Athena the loved goddess of war.

"I am Damos...war personified, rage personified, anger personified.

"I am the boy no one knows but everyone fears. You do not know me. You do not want to know me. You will never know me if I so choose.... All I am is feared and loathed...as I carry the load of every single sin and venal act....

"You think that you see me, but you do not. You think that you hear me, but you will not. You think that you love me, but you do not....

"I am all that is combined in the things you fear most.... You think you understand my threats, but you do not. You think that I am silent and sullied and uncertain, but I am not."

Even as he's secretly fantasizing about bringing cosmic ruin upon his father, Hunter is complaining about being publicly cast as a political liability.

In February 2019, he tells his daughter Naomi that Joe has embarrassed him by saying he can't run for president for family reasons.

"I told Pop the first time he said it to never say it again—'I'm worried about how it will impact the family'...it implies your family (particularly me) will embarrass you.

"Sometimes Pop can't help himself.... His factoring in the family has been simply to gauge whether any of us have screwed up so bad it would diminish his chances.

"You cannot say over and over again that there's nothing any of us have ever done that even impacts the voter in the margins—AND—say that the skeletons of his family may make it hard for him to put us through the wringer in his pursuit of the office....

"He doesn't say it himself that directly anymore, but all of his advisors do.... How he can't see how angry and frustrated it makes you guys to have the world think Pop may be prohibitively barred from the presidency because your Dad is such a fuck up....

"As much as he is running for President the four of us will have to fight for the image we want [to] impress upon the world in the moment and for history."

But ultimately it was Joe's image—not Hunter's—that remained paramount.

In April 2019, according to his lawyer George Mesires, Hunter resigned from the Burisma board so as not to distract from his father's upcoming presidential bid.

"My qualifications and work are being attacked by Rudy Giuliani and his minions for transparent political purposes," Hunter said in a statement at the time.

No doubt severing almost his last remaining reliable source of cash did not come easily and must have added to the deep reservoir of bitterness he held against his father.

That same month Hunter abandoned his laptop in the Delaware repair shop.

In his 2007 memoir, *Promises to Keep*, Joe Biden wrote that he once asked Hunter when he was a boy: "What do you want to be when you grow up?"

"I want to be important," Hunter responded.

The tragedy for Hunter—and the danger for his father—was that he never felt important enough.

The Grift

"I've never focused on money for me."
—Joe Biden, primary debate, February 2020, New Hampshire

Uncle Jim is at the end of his tether with his daughter Caroline in the summer of 2018. In desperation, he turns to Hunter.

The pampered Georgetown graduate has a history of substance abuse and a string of run-ins with police. Now she is facing criminal charges in a New York court after admitting to spending $110,000 on beauty products using a stolen credit card at a Greenwich Village pharmacy.

"I need help with Caroline, she is off the rails," Jim emails Hunter on July 13, 2018.

In the third month of a crack binge in Los Angeles, Hunter might seem a curious choice as mentor, but Caroline hero-worships her dashing cousin, so his job is to keep her out of trouble for ten days until her sentencing in New York.

"I'm babysitting my 32-year-old cousin before she has to go to her sentencing hearing in NYC for felony grand larceny charge," Hunter tells a friend. "She can't fuck up in any way between now and then."

Keeping the lanky blonde on the straight and narrow was easier said than done.

"Hey, if you need me to burn down the Chateau Marmont," she texts him, after listening to his kvetching about being blacklisted from his favorite hotel, "I will, literally and figuratively."

Hunter was going to have his hands full.

The stylish Paris Hilton lookalike had been arrested twice after her uncle became vice president. While living in New York as an art gallery worker she appears to have fallen into the family trap of living beyond her means.

In 2013, after her roommate at her luxury Tribeca apartment confronted her about unpaid rent, the *New York Post* reported, she went on a "violent rampage."

When the NYPD arrived to break up the fight, Caroline was accused of assaulting a female officer, "throwing punches and flailing frantically as cops wrestled her into handcuffs."

"You don't know who I am," she allegedly told them before complaining she couldn't breathe.

She was last seen in photographs that day being carted out of the police station in a wheelchair by paramedics, draped in a white sheet, like an Egyptian mummy, for an ambulance ride to the hospital.

Jim Biden had paid the deposit on the $3,500-a-month apartment Caroline was subletting from a New York University student, whose mother told the *Post*: "If you're an elitist Biden, I guess you think you're owed the world."

Caroline's case reportedly was dismissed after she agreed to attend the luxury Caron Renaissance rehab facility in Florida for "anger management."

She was lucky again in 2018. After her sojourn with Hunter in L.A., she was sentenced in the Manhattan Criminal Court to two years' probation, only to be arrested the following year for driving under the influence, after she crashed her car into a tree near her parents' mansion in Pennsylvania. She copped a plea of twenty days' rehab and five months' probation.

"The problem Caroline has had is that most of her friends are independently wealthy and she has not had a steady work environment that was challenging and engaging," wrote Jim, in an email to Hunter's business partner, James Gilliar, asking for help finding his daughter a high-paying job.

When her dad and Uncle Joe pulled strings for a marketing job in L.A. with a salary of $85,000 plus bonus, Caroline was furious.

"I cannot take this job—I have never made this little money in my life," she emailed Jim. "I cannot survive on this…. Can I counteroffer?"

She griped to Hunter in a text: "I don't want to take this Fucking job…. Your dad told me he was done with me yesterday…. Casey and Missy [her cousins] work at Coke and Starbucks but I'm the untrustworthy black sheep."

While Joe Biden waged war on white privilege from the White House, his own family was the living embodiment of the worst of it.

In 2015, another of Hunter's cousins, Missy Owens, asked him to procure a government appointment for her mother, Joe's sister Val.

Missy, along with her sister Casey, landed a federal job during the Obama administration, before graduating to a high-paying "government relations" job with Coca-Cola. Casey wound up as a vice president of Starbucks.

Missy had spotted a White House press release announcing that Hunter's partner at Rosemont Seneca, Eric Schwerin, had been rewarded with a plum Obama appointment to the Commission for the Preservation of America's Heritage Abroad.

Schwerin had been a Mr. Fix-It for Hunter since the days they worked together in the Clinton Commerce Department.

As president of Rosemont Seneca, he grew close to the Biden family and would do everything for Hunter, from ordering his tax affairs to covering for him when he went AWOL.

Schwerin discreetly managed Joe's financial affairs too. The VP attended his birthday dinner at DC's Graffiato restaurant for twenty minutes in May 2016.

So, if anyone deserved a government sinecure, surely it was Eric!

But Missy had a bee in her bonnet about the appointment.

"Is this our Eric?" she emailed Hunter. "How did he/we find that one, and do you think we can find something for my mom?... I really want to get on something, but mom needs it more than I do right now."

Hunter replied: "I didn't know she wanted to do [one] of these.... Let's go through the list with Steve [Ricchetti, Joe's chief of staff and later White House counselor] and see what makes sense."

Lo and behold, in September 2016, President Obama appointed Aunt Val to a ceremonial role at the United Nations, a four-month stint that paid $26,000.

Schwerin sent Hunter a memo outlining two additional $12,500 per month "consulting" contracts for Aunt Val for when the UN gig ran out, one with the Biden Foundation and the other with the University of Delaware.

Joe's brother Frank Biden, eleven years his junior, is no stranger to the family grift, either.

On the day of Joe's inauguration as president, Frank was featured prominently in a two-page newspaper ad touting his relationship with "my brother" for the South Florida law firm that pays him as an adviser, even though he isn't a lawyer.

He and his wife, Mindy Ward, a Hooters waitress turned American Airlines flight attendant, live in Florida, but when Joe was VP they were regular guests to state dinners and other VIP networking opportunities.

Frank also had run-ins with the law, including a string of DUIs. In October 2003, Frank reportedly was arrested for petty theft after being caught at a Blockbuster video rental store in Pompano Beach, Florida, with DVDs of *Rabbit-Proof Fence* and *They* stuffed down the front of his pants. He was forty-nine years old at the time.

When it came to business, it didn't hurt to have a brother who was VP. For Frank, a lucky break came in 2009, when he was trying to get rich in Costa Rica doing real estate and casino deals.

As the *New York Post* reported, his fortunes rose with the Costa Rican government when Joe flew into town aboard Air Force Two and went to the presidential palace "for a one-on-one with President Oscar Arias."

As it happened, Joe had been deputized as the Obama administration's point man in Latin America and the Caribbean. Funny how that worked.

Joe has always made sure the Bidens lived a life of unearned privilege and entitlement under his beneficent patronage. His children and grandchildren, nieces and nephews, brothers and sister, and a lucky few trusted advisors and their families, would want for nothing. Within the first few months of his presidency, at least five children of his top aides would secure coveted jobs in the new administration, the *Washington Post* reported.

Like members of a hereditary aristocracy, the Bidens would have access to the best America can give, the most prestigious educational institutions, internships, clerkships, scholarships, directorships, and government sinecures.

Investors knocked at their doors, the Secret Service was at their beck and call, and there always was easy entrée into high-paying jobs with corporate donors who craved the favor of the back-slapping senator for Delaware.

Brushes with the law would be smoothed over; bargains would always find them. Life for a Biden was a magic carpet ride gliding over obstacles that trip up mere mortals.

Hunter once described the privilege and the burden of being part of a "great family" to his best friend in business Devon Archer.

Archer had been convicted in 2018 on federal fraud charges with two other men over the Indian tribal bonds scheme.

Archer's co-defendants would go to jail, Bevan Cooney for thirty months and Jason Galanis for sixteen years. But Archer did not. He had the good fortune that his conviction was overturned in November 2019 by US District Court Judge Ronnie Abrams, an Obama appointee.

In October 2020, a federal appeals court reversed Abrams's decision and reinstated the conviction, declaring the District Court had "abused its discretion in vacating the judgement." Archer has appealed to the Supreme Court.

In the middle of these legal machinations, he had a moment of doubt.

"Why did your dad's administration appointees arrest me and try and put me in jail?" he texted Hunter on March 6, 2019. "Just curious…

"Why would they try and ruin my family and destroy my kids and no one from your family's side step in and at least try to help me? I don't get it….

"Bunch of these Asians getting in my head asking me the same so just curious what I should answer…. I'm depressed I love you anyway."

Hunter gave him a mini-lecture about democracy and co-equal branches of government. And then he got to the point.

"Every great family is persecuted…you are part of a great family—not a side show, not deserted by them even in your darkest moments. That's the way Bidens are different, and you are a Biden. It's the price of power and the people questioning you truly have none."

Cafe Milano

"I've never spoken to my son about his overseas business dealings."
—Joe Biden, September 2019, Des Moines, Iowa

Cafe Milano is a Georgetown institution renowned less for its grilled calamari and velvety burrata than for its discretion. The restaurant's catchphrase is: "Where the world's most powerful people go," and that was the case one balmy evening in April 2015, when Hunter organized for his father to meet a group of his foreign business associates for dinner in a private room.

Hunter was busy in the spring of 2015. He and Kathleen had started marriage counseling. He had been traveling the world, on behalf of Chinese energy company CEFC, the capitalist arm of President Xi Jinping's Belt and Road Initiative.

The Biden family was enjoying the perks of Joe's office, now in his second term as vice president. Money was starting to roll in.

But Hunter's foreign clients were pressuring him to meet Joe, and it was increasingly difficult to organize visits to the West Wing. President Obama's office was watching, and the White House counsel had started to put up roadblocks.

So, Hunter decided to organize a dinner off-site and kill three birds with one stone. His father could meet his benefactors from Ukraine, Kazakhstan, and Russia at the same time in the same place.

The dinner was held on April 16, 2015, in Cafe Milano's private "Garden Room."

The next day, Hunter received an email from Vadym Pozharskyi, a senior executive of the corrupt Ukrainian energy company Burisma, to thank him for introducing him to his father.

"Dear Hunter, thank you for inviting me to DC and giving an opportunity to meet your father and spent [*sic*] some time together," Pozharskyi wrote on April 17.

"It's realty [*sic*] an honor and pleasure."

At the time, Burisma was paying Hunter $83,333 a month to sit on its board.

Hunter told guests before the dinner that his father would be there. In one email, he appears to use his role on the board of World Food Program USA as a cover story for the evening's true purpose of introducing his father to his business associates.

"Ok—the reason for the dinner is ostensibly to discuss food security," writes Hunter on March 26 to Michael Karloutsos, with whom he had been discussing a business deal in Greece involving eco-friendly trains from China.

"Dad will be there but keep that between us for now. Thanks."

Karloutsos replies: "Everything is between us. All good"!... I know you mentioned your dad would probably join the dinner as well."

The guest list prepared by Hunter three weeks before the dinner included Russian billionaire Yelena Baturina and her husband, corrupt former Moscow mayor Yury Luzhkov, who since has died.

Baturina had wired $3.5 million on February 14, 2014, to Rosemont Seneca Thornton LLC, a consortium formed between Rosemont

Seneca—the firm cofounded by Hunter, Archer, and Heinz—and the Boston-based Thornton Group, to pursue a Chinese joint venture.

Baturina's wires were flagged in suspicious activity reports provided by the Treasury Department to a Senate Republican inquiry by the Finance and Homeland Security and Governmental Affairs Committees, chaired by Senators Chuck Grassley and Ron Johnson.

Three officials from Kazakhstan also were invited to the Cafe Milano dinner, including Marc Holtzman, then chairman of the former Soviet republic's largest bank, Kazkommertsbank.

A Mexican ambassador and representatives of World Food Program USA were included on the guest list, which Hunter emailed to Archer three weeks before the dinner:

"3 seats for our KZ [Kazakhstan] friends," he wrote.

"2 seats for Yelana [*sic*] and husband.

"2 [seats for] you and me.

"3 seats for WFPUSA people.

"Vadym [Pozharskyi, Burisma executive].

"3 Ambassadors (MX, ?, ?).

"Total 14."

The laptop does not record if everyone on Hunter's list attended.

Archer emailed Hunter before the event to say that Baturina did not want to come but her husband Luzhkov would attend.

"Yelena doesn't want to steal Yuri's [sic] thunder, so she'll be in town to meet with us but doesn't want to come to dinner," Archer wrote on March 20. "That was just her thoughts. We could insist."

He finished: "Obviously save a seat for your guy (and mine if he's in town)."

Hunter replied: "I think your guy being there is more trouble than it's worth—unless you have some other idea."

It's unclear if Archer's "guy" was John Kerry or someone else.

Rick Leach, founder of World Food Program USA, emailed Hunter at 11:15 p.m. to thank him after the dinner: "What a fantastic and productive evening—thank you!"

Kazakhstan banker Holtzman emailed: "Deer [sic] Hunter, Thank you for an amazing evening, wonderful company and great conversation. I look forward to seeing you soon and to many opportunities to work closely together."

Hunter does not name the other two Kazakhstan representatives on his guest list, but an unverified photograph posted on anti-corruption website Kazakhstani Initiative on Asset Recovery in 2019 offers a clue.

A smiling Joe Biden and Hunter are seen alongside Kazakhstan's then-Prime Minister Karim Massimov and junior oligarch Kenes Rakishev, thirty-four, in the photograph, which appears to have been taken that night at the Cafe Milano.

Contemporaneous online photos of the interior of the restaurant match the background of the shot, and a faint image of the Cafe Milano logo can be seen through a sheer curtain behind Hunter's head. Joe has taken off his tie, as have the two Kazakhstanis.

Further corroboration comes from an email inviting Archer to a "small private breakfast" on the morning of the dinner in the Massimov's suite at the Willard Hotel: "There are several matters the Prime Minister is eager to discuss with you and he will be grateful for the opportunity to spend quality time together."

The following year, Hunter will describe Massimov in an email as a "close friend."

Hunter and Archer's chummy correspondence with Rakishev, who pitches money-making ideas, and asks for a meeting with John Kerry, also appears on the laptop. Rakishev calls Hunter "my brother from another mother."

The junior Kazakhstan oligarch, estimated by Forbes to be worth $332 million, was the main shareholder of Kazkommertsbank.

His company Novatus used a Latvian bank to wire $142,300 to Archer's firm, Rosemont Seneca Bohai, on April 22, 2014, according to a currency transaction report recorded in the Grassley-Johnson Senate report. The wire included a note saying the money was "for a car."

Since the *New York Post* first reported, in October 2020, on the Pozharskyi email from Hunter's abandoned laptop, thanking Hunter for the meeting with his father, the White House has not responded to the paper's inquiries. It has not disputed the accuracy of the paper's stories about the laptop, nor requested a retraction or correction.

The Biden campaign told *USA Today*, in December 2020, that it "categorically denied a meeting ever happened."

"The Biden campaign, after a comprehensive review, had said a meeting never took place between Joe Biden and Pozharskyi," wrote Glenn Kessler, the *Washington Post* fact-checker.

But in June 2021, after the *New York Post* published further details of the meeting, including that it was a dinner where Joe met multiple business associates of Hunter's, the White House came clean.

After eight months of denials and stonewalling, an unnamed "White House individual with knowledge of Joe Biden's schedules" told Kessler that the VP did go to Cafe Milano that night but "only dropped by briefly to meet with one of the guests" and "there was no discussion of politics or business."

But of course, that's not how it works. Joe just has to show up and shake hands. All that matters is that Hunter demonstrates his pulling power.

The White House source claimed that Joe's attendance was not listed on his official schedule because he only decided to "drop by" at the last minute "after the schedule was completed."

Yet Hunter had been telling his guests for three weeks that his father would be at the dinner.

The White House also attempted to put a religious gloss on the dinner, via Kessler, claiming Joe only went to Cafe Milano to see Father Alex Karloutsos, who was at the dinner with his son Michael.

"Joe Biden, a Roman Catholic, also has a long history of working with the Greek Orthodox Church."

It's a weirdly byzantine explanation for why Joe was there at all, but in the end, the *Washington Post* story serves to confirm that Hunter had introduced Pozharskyi to his father, contradicting Joe's denials of any knowledge of Hunter's overseas business dealings.

10

Breakfast of Billionaires

*"I've looked at what your family has done and
want to follow in that tradition."*
**—Hunter to Miguel Magnani, grandson of a
former Mexican president, February 2016**

"Breakfast with Dad—NavObs" was the diary entry for 8:30 a.m. on November 19, 2015.

Mexican billionaire Carlos Slim was in Washington, DC, as Politico noted the next day: "SPOTTED: Carlos Slim in the lobby yesterday morning of the Georgetown Four Seasons."

So was his fellow Mexican tycoon Miguel Alemán Velasco and his forty-nine-year-old son, Miguel Alemán Magnani, the founder of budget airline Interjet, at whose Acapulco mansion Hunter and wife, Kathleen, had stayed that March.

Jeff Cooper, a long-time Biden family benefactor, who had been working frantically with Hunter on energy deals in Mexico, was in town as well.

What a coincidence that all four of Hunter's business associates found themselves having breakfast with his father that morning at the vice presidential residence at Number One Observatory Circle in the grounds of the US Naval Observatory, or NavObs, for short.

Five photographs date-stamped on that day and taken at 10:03 a.m. and 10:04 a.m. appear on Hunter's laptop, showing Joe and Hunter posing with the four visitors.

The photos were taken in the living room, which was painted at the time in a daffodil yellow chosen by Jill Biden and featured distinctive paintings by Vermont artist Wolf Kahn on loan from a gallery in Georgetown, which are visible on the wall behind the men. Two floral chairs and a pink-toned silk rug in the photos match the decor of the living room at the time.

Joe Biden insists he never knew a thing about Hunter's lucrative deals in countries where he wielded influence as vice president.

But evidence abounds on the laptop of Joe's active participation. Among more than one hundred events scheduled in Hunter's diary at NavObs there are meetings that overlap with Hunter's business interests.

Joe met with Hunter's business associates in his office in the West Wing. He took his son on Air Force Two to countries where Hunter was doing deals and, on at least one occasion, included one of Hunter's business partners, on the trip.

Hunter's involvement with Carlos Slim, at one time the world's richest man, commenced soon after a White House state dinner the magnate attended in May 2010, along with Joe and Jill, to honor Mexican President Felipe Calderón.

Eva Longoria, Beyonce, and former CIA boss John Brennan also attended.

The charmed path that always opened for Hunter when his father met a foreign leader or oligarch led him to Mexico on a VIP trip the following year.

Hunter's diary in May 2011 shows a "tentative tour hosted by Carlos Slim" of the tycoon's private Museo Soumaya in Mexico City, which Slim founded and named after his late wife, Soumaya Domit. Containing priceless sculptures from pre-Hispanic Mesoamerica, there could be no greater honor offered to Hunter than a private tour with the billion-aire founder.

Hunter also had breakfast with Slim's friend, Mexican billionaire Carlos Bremer, at his magnificent villa in Monterrey. Bremer, former director of the country's stock exchange, had donated millions of dollars to the Clinton Foundation and sat on the foundation's board.

Hunter subsequently would hold in-person and video conference meetings with Slim's sons, Carlos Jr. and Tony Slim.

He would visit Mexico again in 2012, 2013, 2014, and 2015. His final recorded visit was with his father and Cooper aboard Air Force 2.

"Miguel wants us to go to Mexico City," Cooper wrote to Hunter on February 26, 2013. "This is setting up to be flippin gigantic brother."

At the time, President Enrique Peña Nieto was reforming Mexico's energy market to allow private capital investment in state-owned oil and gas monopoly Petróleos Mexicanos (Pemex).

Uncle Jim Biden, Joe's younger brother, also was keen on leveraging the family's connection with the "very friendly" Carlos Slim.

He emailed Hunter on May 7, 2015, about a deal that would involve Slim and Pemex.

"Have a very real deal with Pemex (Carlos Slim) need financing lit-erally for a few days to a week," he wrote.

Hunter and Cooper also were hoping for the Slim family's money for Cooper's online gaming company and digital wallet firm ePlata, in which Hunter had a 5 percent stake through his firm Owasco.

"Just wondering who is the best first major partner outside [the Alemáns'] Interjet. Obviously Slims provide that if we could actually sell them on the idea and not have them just take it and create their own," Hunter emailed Cooper in February 2015.

"Spoke to my dad about 'Slim ask,'" Hunter wrote Cooper in a later text message.

"Oh that sounds SO F'ING GOOD," replied Cooper.

Cooper joined the VP's entourage on Air Force Two to Mexico in 2016, when he and Hunter were trying to negotiate an ill-fated petroleum deal with Alemán Magnani.

At 6:00 p.m. on February 24, 2016, about an hour after "wheels up" from Joint Base Andrews on the five-hour flight to Mexico City, Hunter wrote a plaintive email to Alemán Magnani using Air Force Two's secure, high-speed satellite communications channel. He blind-copied Cooper.

"We are arriving late tonight on Air Force 2 to Mx City. I'm attending meeting w/ President N [Peña Nieto] and dad. Would love to see you but you never respond. I am really upset by it…. I want you at the plane when the VP lands with your Mom and Dad and you completely ignore me.

"I've looked at what your family has done and want to follow in that tradition…. We have been talking about business deals for 7 years. And I really appreciate you letting me stay at your resort villa…but I have brought every single person you have ever asked me to bring to the F'ing White House and the Vice President's house and the inauguration and then you go completely silent…. You make me feel like I've done something to offend you." Hunter had been useful to Alemán Magnani. There were meetings with his dad and three tickets for his family to the Obama-Biden inauguration ball in 2013.

Crucially for a Mexican airline owner wanting to spread his wings, Hunter also set up two meetings for Alemán Magnani with Secretary of Transportation Anthony Foxx, on March 17, 2014, and January 23, 2015, and a separate meeting with the administrator of the Federal Aviation Authority, emails on the laptop show.

When Cooper asked if he would go to the first Foxx meeting Hunter replied: "No, but I am calling Sec. Foxx to let him know we are buddies."

Before the second meeting, Hunter emailed Foxx's director of scheduling and advance, Laura De Castro: "Miguel Aleman (Interjet Chairman) is a close family friend, but I have no business with the company."

Burisma, the corrupt Ukrainian energy company that was paying Hunter $83,333 to sit on its board, also got involved in his Mexican ventures.

In a 2014 email Cooper wrote to Hunter: "I met with Miguel [Alemán Magnani] last night. He has set up mtgs with the Secty of Energy and the CEO of Pemex for Jan 12. Is there any chance that anyone from Burisma could attend?"

Hunter later asked Alemán Magnani to intervene with the Mexican government to "smooth out" a visa problem for Burisma's owner Mykola Zlochevsky. Alemán Magnani does not appear to have assisted.

As a result, Zlochevsky could not fly to Mexico to finalize a deal Cooper had brokered with Pemex, thus jeopardizing one of Hunter's most profitable side hustles.

"Going to have to do some serious back pedaling with Burisma," Hunter emailed Cooper on February 16, 2015. "Most likely jeopardizes my board position."

"I am shocked Miguel didn't come through at crunch time," replied Cooper."…they clearly value the relationship with your family AND they know they could sustain serious damage here by making enemies with you…. Maybe a call from you or your dad to his dad? Maybe that shakes things loose. Whaddya think?"

No reply can be found on the laptop, but Hunter knows that his arrival with Dad on Air Force Two the following year will demonstrate his clout to prospective Mexican business partners.

Nothing "shakes things lose" abroad quite so profitably as jetting in on the White House bird.

11

Burisma

S ix months after Joe was sworn in as vice president in 2009, Hunter, then thirty-nine, founded his investment firm, Rosemont Seneca Partners. His partners were Chris Heinz, thirty-six, the stepson of Senator John Kerry, and Heinz's best friend from Yale, Devon Archer, thirty-five, a former senior advisor to Kerry.

Archer would later be convicted over a $60 million scheme to defraud an American Indian tribe, but in those early days he was the golden boy of their trio.

A charming interloper among the moneyed elites he met at Yale, Archer grew up on Long Island, the son of a Vietnam veteran turned realtor. He was "handsome and very charming, with an easy smile," said someone who knew him at college. "He got a lot of positive feedback for his interpersonal skills."

He would marry Krista, a Manhattan podiatrist; have three kids; move to a $3.6 million townhouse in Brooklyn; and buy an eight-bedroom $3.7 million lakefront in Quogue, Long Island, three years before his 2018 conviction in a Manhattan federal court. Summers were spent at the Swordfish Beach Club in Westhampton and the Plandome Country Club in Manhasset.

Archer was a hard worker, but while he saw himself as an investor, colleagues said his skills were better suited to sales and marketing. He and Hunter were regarded as "naïve" about the private equity world and wanted to make money quickly, which led Archer to take greater and greater risks.

On April 16, 2014, he appeared in a photograph taken with Joe at the White House that would haunt the vice president in the years to come.

It shows Joe and Archer smiling broadly for the camera in front of an American flag in the VP's West Wing office. It was just one week before Archer would join the board of Ukrainian energy company Burisma.

The photo was posted on the Burisma website the next day, which presumably was the point.

The White House never disputed the authenticity of the photo but suggested, via proxies, that the meeting was to help Archer's seven-year-old son, Luke, with a school "art project." Archer described it differently two weeks earlier in an email to Hunter: "Any word on Luke book report meeting WH [White House]?"

The same day that the vice president invited Burisma's newest board member into the White House, almost 4,000 miles away in London's Central Criminal Court, the UK's Serious Fraud Office was granted an order to freeze $23 million in the British bank accounts of Burisma's oligarch owner, Mykola Zlochevsky, as part of a joint MI5-FBI corruption investigation into former members of the kleptocrat government of ousted pro-Russian president Viktor Yanukovych.

Five days later, Joe flew to Kyiv, promising millions in US aid for a fragile Ukraine. The US-backed Maidan revolution in February had successfully removed Yanukovych, but Russia had responded by annexing Crimea, and a bloody civil war was raging in Eastern Ukraine against pro-Russian separatists. An interim government was in place until elections in May, which would be won by an ebullient oligarch nicknamed the "Chocolate King," the US/Europe-aligned Petro Poroshenko.

On May 12, 2014, Hunter joined Archer on the Burisma board, for the handsome sum of $83,333 per month.

Years later, the *Washington Post*'s David Ignatius would acknowledge that the White House photograph with Archer had done Joe reputational harm by linking him to Burisma.

"The danger that Hunter Biden's Burisma connection might be misused was illustrated [when] Burisma posted a photograph on its website of Devon Archer, Hunter Biden's business partner, standing with the then-vice president before an American flag at what appeared to be the White House," he wrote in October 2020.

Ignatius quoted an unnamed consultant, who urged Hunter through a friend "to have Burisma take down the photo, and it was removed from the company's website that day."

The claim is confirmed by an email, on May 13, 2014, to Hunter and Archer asking them urgently to take down the photo, on the request of Demetra Lambros, the vice president's chief counsel.

"Hey. Guys. There is apparently a photo of Devon and the VP on Burisma's website," wrote Hunter's fixer, Eric Schwerin. "Demetra called and asked that we tell Burisma they need to take it down (legally they aren't comfortable with the VP's picture being up on the site as what seems like an endorsement)."

Joe would meet with Zlochevsky's envoy, Vadym Pozharskyi, thirty-six, at the Cafe Milano dinner in April 2015.

A sign that Hunter's value to Burisma lay in his father's power came ten weeks after Joe ceased to be vice president, when Hunter's monthly director's fee was cut in half from April 2017.

In an email on March 19, 2017, Pozharskyi asked Hunter to sign a new director's agreement and informed him "the only thing that was amended is the compensation rate...

"The remuneration is still the highest in the company and higher than the standard director's monthly fees. I am sure you will find it both fair and reasonable."

From then on, the amount listed on Hunter's Burisma invoices was reduced to $41,500, paid in euros.

As soon as Hunter and Archer were signed up to the Burisma board, Pozharskyi wasted no time pressuring them to use their influence in Washington to help his boss, Zlochevsky, forty-seven, escape the international criminal probe that was closing in.

While his father was visiting Kyiv, on April 22, 2014, Hunter sent an email to Archer titled "JRB in UKR," with a quote from Joe's speech to the Ukrainian parliament: "Mr Biden spoke of the 'humiliating threats' faced by Ukraine and said the United States was 'ready to assist.' But he also stressed that Ukraine needs to…reduce its crippling dependence on Russia for supplies of natural gas."

"Wow," replied Archer. "We need to make sure this rag tag temporary government in the Ukraine understands the value of Burisma to its very existence."

Hunter tells him: "You should send to Vadim [*sic*]—makes it look like we are adding value."

In truth, Hunter had been working for weeks on a strategy to leverage his father's influence for maximum value with Burisma.

The week before Joe's Kyiv trip, Hunter urged Archer to expedite the Burisma arrangement. "The contract should begin now—not after the upcoming visit of my guy," he wrote on April 13.

"The announcement of my guy's upcoming travels should be characterized as part of our advice and thinking—but what he will say and do is out of our hands."

Earlier that month, Hunter and Archer had flown to Italy's Lake Como for a two-day "workshop" on financial markets run by the prestigious Ambrosetti Club, which previously had hosted his father. They stayed at the sumptuous hotel favored by oligarchs, Villa d'Este, on the lake's edge. On April 3, Hunter had a private meeting scheduled with fellow Ambrosetti guest Stephen Schwarzman, the billionaire chairman of the Blackstone Group.

The following day he went to the hotel's terrace bar to meet Russia's richest woman, Elena Baturina, the wife of the corrupt former mayor of Moscow, who had just wired $3.5 million to a bank account associated with Archer at Rosemont Seneca Thornton.

In emails before meeting the Russian oligarch, Archer and Hunter compared themselves to fictional spies, James Bond and Jason Bourne: "Might be very Bond/Bourne to get the gharchs [oligarchs] up at the lake for a meeting;)," wrote Archer.

It is not known if they met with Ukrainian oligarch Zlochevsky at Lake Como, but at some point during the visit, they did catch up with his envoy Pozharskyi, who referred to their meeting in an email on May 12 in which he asked that they "use your influence" to combat the Ukrainian government's allegations against Burisma of "misappropriation, embezzlement or conversion of property by malversation."

"Following our talks during the visit to the Como Lake and our further discussions, I would like to bring the following situation to your attention" wrote Pozharskyi. "One or more pretrial proceedings were initiated by the Ministry of Internal Affairs with regard to Burisma Holdings companies....

"We urgently need your advice on how you could use your influence to convey a message/signal, etc to stop what we consider to be politically motivated actions."

Hunter replied: "Vadim—I am with Devon in Doha. We will have a discussion with the [lawyers] Boies Schiller team ASAP."

Boies is the New York–based law firm that paid Hunter $216,000 a year as "of counsel," and whose chairman is long-time Joe donor and super-lawyer David Boies. In another email with Archer, Hunter stressed that Burisma must pay $25,000 per month as a retainer to Boies, "for our protection."

Pozharskyi was even more demanding in his reply to Hunter on May 12, 2014.

He named two members of the interim Ukrainian government who could intervene to end the "attacks" on Burisma: "Prime Minister [Arseniy] Yatseniuk or acting President [Oleksandr] Turchinov" could 'communicate a request to Acting Minister [Arsen] Avakov to stop that.'"

Avakov was the minister of internal affairs who controlled Ukraine's national law enforcement agency.

Hunter seemed not to worry that he was being asked to exert political influence through his father on the fragile interim government of Ukraine, two weeks before its presidential election, to benefit a corrupt business that was paying him $1 million a year.

He forwarded Pozharskyi's emails to Boies's lawyer, Heather King, who replied that afternoon: "The immediate plan is to reach out to the Energy and Ukraine desks, respectively, at State Dept to…'update' them on Burisma's current situation…. We can't just go in there with a hard ask but it is often the case that the conversation is open to an ask, assuming it goes well.

"That will include an outreach to Carlos Pascual, the top US energy diplomat…at State. He was formerly Ambassador to Ukraine."

Pascual quit the State Department three months later to go into private practice.

King also suggested they "engage a lobbyist…. I don't want to register under the lobbying disclosure act or the foreign agents registration act." She suggested Secretary of State Kerry's former chief of staff, Washington lobbyist David Leiter. "He is very close with Sec. Kerry."

Just before Christmas 2014, Zlochevsky managed to escape the clutches of UK's Serious Fraud Office, thanks to shenanigans in Ukraine's prosecutor general's office. Someone in the office had signed a letter, dated December 2, 2014, which claimed that Zlochevsky "was not suspected of any crime," the *Guardian* reported.

That letter appeared to be crucial in a British judge's decision to rule against the Serious Fraud Squad. The case against Zlochevsky collapsed, and he got back his $23 million.

Ukraine's prosecutor general at the time was an ex-cop, Vitaly Yarema.

George Kent, a US embassy official in Kyiv, would tell the US Justice Department that Burisma had paid a $7 million bribe to Ukrainian prosecutors sometime between May and December 2014 to kill the investigation, according to investigative journalist John Solomon from Just the News.

In a State Department memo, Kent wrote that Yarema's team "closed the case against Zlochevsky…just before western Christmas Day…after the FBI and MI-5 spent months and arguably millions working to try to put together the first possible asset recovery case against [Zlochevsky over alleged] bribes paid for the licenses issued for gas oil permits."

Kent wrote that Yarema was "responsible for the outrage." After a fiery meeting with Kent and another US official in February 2015, Yarema quit as chief prosecutor.

Now Zlochevsky, living in exile in Monte Carlo, was off the hook in London.

But he would face new problems in Ukraine with Yarema's replacement, Viktor Shokin, a sixty-two-year-old former prosecutor of modest means who was brought out of retirement by the new president, Poroshenko, to take over as Ukraine's prosecutor general on February 10, 2015.

<hr />

Disquiet was bubbling away inside the US State Department over Hunter's entanglement with Zlochevsky, who was banned from entering the country.

The Obama administration's new special envoy on energy policy, Israel-born Amos Hochstein, forty-two, had taken over in August 2014. He tried twice to raise concerns about Hunter's Burisma role, including directly with Joe in the West Wing in October 2015.

"I wanted to make sure that he was aware that there was an increase in chatter on media outlets close to Russians and corrupt oligarch-owned media outlets [about] Hunter Biden being part of the board of Burisma," he testified to the Grassley-Johnson inquiry.

After Holstein confronted Joe, Hunter contacted him to say his father had said they should meet.

On November 6, 2015, Hunter's diary shows he met Hochstein at Le Pain Quotidien in Georgetown, near his office. Hochstein told him that "the Russians were using his name in order to sow disinformation… among Ukrainians."

On November 12, Hunter's secretary left him a message that Hochstein had called: "Please call back today, if possible."

On December 7, 2015, Hochstein tried again to raise the issue with Joe on Air Force 2 on a flight to Ukraine, but his pleas were ignored.

Hochstein wasn't the only US State Department official concerned that Hunter's Burisma role undermined the US anti-corruption message. The Kyiv embassy's Kent had gone to the VP's office in February 2015, when he first heard about Hunter's connection to the "odious oligarch" Zlochevsky.

"I raised my concern that Hunter Biden's status as a [Burisma] board member could create the perception of a conflict of interest," Kent testified to the Senate inquiry.

"I thought that someone needed to talk to Hunter Biden, and he should [step] down from the board of Burisma." But Kent never heard back from Joe's office.

In the middle of this consternation at the State Department, on May 22, 2015, Hunter emailed one of his father's most trusted advisers, Deputy Secretary of State Tony Blinken (whom Joe would appoint Secretary of State in 2021) to ask if he had "a few minutes next week to grab a cup of coffee?…would like to get your advice on a couple of things."

"Absolutely.… Look forward to seeing you," replied Blinken.

The meeting was scheduled for May 27, 2015, and Hunter was told he would be ushered through "the diplomatic entrance of the State Department."

Due to Beau's worsening health, they rescheduled for July 22. Blinken testified to the Grassley-Johnson inquiry that he couldn't remember the conversation, except that "we talked about his brother, about the effect it was having on the family [and] Vice President Biden. It was all about the loss the family had suffered and how they were coping."

Blinken also claimed he had no idea Hunter was on Burisma's board and said no one raised concerns with him.

As the Ukrainian prosecutors' probe into Zlochevsky gathered pace toward the end of 2015, Pozharskyi ratcheted up the pressure on Hunter and Archer, explicitly demanding that they use their influence to "close down" the criminal investigation against Burisma.

He wanted "a list of deliverables...a concrete course of actions, incl. meetings/communications resulting in high-ranking US officials in Ukraine (US Ambassador) and in US publicly or in private communication/comment expressing their 'positive opinion' and support of Nikolay [Zlochevsky]/Burisma to the highest level of decision makers here in Ukraine: President of Ukraine, president Chief of staff, Prosecutor General, etc," he wrote in an email on November 2, 2015.

"The scope of work should also include organization of a visit of a number of widely recognized and influential current and/or former US policy-makers to Ukraine in November, aiming to conduct meetings with and bring positive signal/message and support on Nikolay's issue to the Ukrainian top officials above with the ultimate purpose to close down any cases/pursuits against Nikolay in Ukraine."

The following month, Joe flew to Kyiv and again addressed the Ukrainian parliament on December 8, 2015. He slammed the "cancer of corruption" in the country and declared: "The Office of the General Prosecutor desperately needs reform."

Behind the scenes, he was pressuring Poroshenko to fire Prosecutor General Shokin.

The reason—according to Joe, the State Department, American media outlets, and the Soros-funded activist group, the Anti-Corruption Action Center—was that Shokin was corrupt, was obstructing reform, and had let the criminal case against Zlochevsky go dormant.

But the opposite was the case.

Shokin was aggressively investigating Burisma, as Pozharskyi had been telling Hunter and Archer in increasingly urgent emails and as contemporaneous news sources in Ukraine would report.

On February 2, 2016, Shokin issued warrants for Zlochevsky's arrest and seized all "movable and immovable property" belonging to him, including four large houses, two plots of land, and "a Rolls-Royce Phantom car," reported the *Kyiv Post*, Interfax-Ukraine, and the National Radio Company.

Ten days later, Joe phoned President Poroshenko.

Five days after the call, Shokin effectively was fired, although it took another month for the Ukrainian parliament to ratify his ousting.

In a leaked recording of a conversation between Poroshenko and Joe on February 18, 2016, the Ukrainian president says he has "good news for you. Yesterday I went to meet with the general prosecutor's office and, in spite of the fact that we don't have any corruption charges, we don't have any information about him doing something wrong, I especially asked him...to resign in his position as a state person, and despite of the fact that he has support in the public. And as a finish of my meeting with him, he promise me to give me the statement of resignation, and one hour ago he bring me the written statement of his resignation."

Joe lets out a sigh and says: "Great."

On May 13, 2016, Joe tells Poroshenko: "Congratulations on getting the new prosecutor general.... It's going to be critical for him to work quickly to repair the damage Shokin did, and I'm a man of my word, and now that the new prosecutor general is in place we're ready to move forward in signing that new one-billion-dollar loan guarantee."

Poroshenko: "Thank you very much indeed for these words of support. Believe me that it was a very tough challenge."

Nine months later, under Shokin's successor as prosecutor general, the politician Yuriy Lutsenko, all legal proceedings against Zlochevsky and Burisma were dropped.

In a speech at the Council on Foreign Relations in 2018, Joe boasted that he had flown into Kyiv and threatened to withhold $1 billion in US loan guarantees for Ukraine unless Shokin was fired.

"I looked at them and said, 'I'm leaving in six hours. If the prosecutor is not fired, you're not getting the money.' Well, son of a bitch. He got fired."

Shokin insists that he was pressured to resign precisely because he was pursuing Zlochevsky and seizing his assets.

In a bombshell interview with Ukrainian publication *Strana* in 2019, he said he had been planning "to interrogate [Hunter] Biden Jr., Archer and so on" before he was ousted.

"The president told me repeatedly that [Joe] Biden demanded that I be removed.... Biden took it very seriously. He promised Poroshenko that he would bring corrupt compromise to me."

At first, Shokin says, "I did not understand the hints that we need to stop investigating Burisma.... All subsequent events are a consequence of my refusal.

"There were regular ultimatums and discussions about me. I finally crossed the threshold on February 2, 2016, when we went to the courts with petitions [to seize] Burisma property. I suppose that then the president received another call from Biden, [threatening] non-allocation of aid.... That's where Poroshenko gave up."

Since Shokin went back into retirement he has been busy trying to clear his name.

When he heard Joe boasting that "he dismissed me and...actively interfered in managerial decision-making at the highest level in Ukraine. I felt that he humiliated not only our president, but the whole of Ukraine."

In April 2020, the Kyiv District Court ordered that Shokin be formally recorded as the victim of an alleged crime by the former US vice president. Joe's identity originally was redacted, but the court ruled that he be formally named.

———◆◆◆———

In his five years on the Burisma teat, until April 2019, Hunter earned $4 million in board fees.

He wrote in his memoir that Burisma's payments were a "wicked sort of funny money" that encouraged him to go on benders for months on end.

By taking a job with Burisma, the hapless Hunter also found himself at the center of a titanic struggle between the US and Russia over energy. It would not be the last time he bumbled into a geopolitical powder keg.

How the vice president's son got involved with such a shady operation always has been obscured by conflicting explanations from Hunter and his minders.

His lawyer George Mesires said that the former Polish president, Aleksander Kwasniewski, a Burisma board member, made the recommendation.

Alan Apter, an American investment banker who served as the board's chairman, told the *Wall Street Journal* he met Archer through mutual friends and then invited him and Hunter to join Burisma, "totally based on merit."

An alternative story is told in the laptop.

Hunter had paid a "finder's fee" to a man named "Alex" for securing him the board position, a 2016 email reveals. The total amount he paid Alex was $277,775, one-third of his Burisma payment for ten months.

So, who was this mysterious Alex? It turns out he was a very interesting link to Hunter's Russian associates.

Alex Kotlarsky was a New York–based Eastern European employed by consulting firm TriGlobal Strategic Ventures, whose website says it helps "Western clients in furthering their business interests in the emerging economies of the former Soviet Union."

TriGlobal's founding partner is Armenian-born Moscow oligarch Ara Abramyan, a close ally of Vladimir Putin—who awarded him one of Russia's highest civilian honors, the Order of Merit to the Fatherland.

Abramyan's sixtieth birthday party in 2017 at a banquet hall near the Kremlin showed how plugged in he is to Putin. Senior government leaders showed up, including Foreign Affairs minister Sergey Lavrov, as seen in photographs on his personal website. A tribute from Putin was read to guests.

Abramyan lived in an $80 million mansion in the upscale Odintsovsky District of West Moscow, across the street from Putin's right-hand man Igor Sechin, the head of Russian state oil conglomerate Rosneft, who will feature in Hunter's misadventures in China.

The plot thickens when you find that Hunter had breakfast with Abramyan at his Moscow home on February 16, 2012. He flew to Russia straight after a lunch in Washington with then-Chinese vice president Xi Jinping.

Hunter's diary entry for February 16 shows "breakfast board of directors 'troika dialog,' lunch w Ara Abramyan his home."

That afternoon he had a meeting with Sergey Chemezov, one of Putin's closest allies and the head of state corporation Rostec. Dinner was with another oligarch. After breakfast the next day back at Abramyan's mansion, there were meetings with two more billionaires.

How Hunter managed to secure access into Russia's oligarch elite is a mystery. But we know that Kotlarsky, Abramyan's underling at TriGlobal, introduced Hunter to Burisma's owner Zlochevsky, because that's what Hunter told the *New Yorker*.

Kotlarsky is described in the 2019 article as a "Ukrainian who was in the car-service business in New York City."

But he appears to have had a significant role in Burisma. He is copied into Hunter and Archer's correspondence with the company and used to fly with Hunter, a row behind him in first class.

The first mention of Kotlarsky on the laptop is June 11, 2012, when he is copied on an email from Archer about a private jet charter to Almaty, Kazakhstan. Burisma would strike a deal in 2014 with Kazakhstan's state-owned energy company, KazMunayGas, to jointly develop oil and gas resources. Hunter and Archer travelled to the former Soviet republic at least three times, including with Zlochevsky, to meet Prime Minister Karim Massimov.

Also with them on that 2012 charter flight to Kazakhstan was Abramyan's partner, Vitaly Pruss, the president of TriGlobal in New York, and a friend of Zlochevsky who once represented the Russian state-owned oil pipeline Transneft.

Hunter liked to say that Burisma was in the noble business of helping Ukraine gain energy independence from Russia. Yet all the people who introduced him to Burisma were aligned with Russia, and Burisma's owner, Zlochevsky, was the former ecology minister under the Russia-aligned President Yanukovych, who fled to exile in Moscow.

CHAPTER

Princelings

"China is going to eat our lunch? Come on, man…. They're not bad folks, folks. But guess what? They're not competition for us."
—Joe Biden, Iowa, 2019

Hunter Biden's trip to Beijing aboard Air Force Two in 2013, accompanying his father on an official visit to see the newly elevated President Xi Jinping, was an unmistakable signal to his Chinese business partners that he was a player in the big game.

He was the American equivalent of a beast they knew very well, a "princeling," anointed as proxy, messenger, and bagman for a powerful family member.

China's princelings are the offspring of China's original communist revolutionary heroes who enrich themselves and their families through an elaborate system of nepotism and cronyism, holding senior positions in state-owned enterprises or becoming high-ranked politicians. They are China's new aristocracy, rich and powerful clans drawn from the top Communist Party cadres through birth or marriage.

By 2021 Forbes reported that 626 Chinese billionaires had a collective net worth of $2.5 trillion, but that figure didn't include the enormous, concealed wealth of the "princelings," gained corruptly or "quasi-legally." Credit Suisse estimated in 2014 that these hidden riches, stashed in tax havens such as the British Virgin Islands and the Cayman Islands, amounted to $1.4 trillion, or about 30 percent of China's gross domestic product.

The so-called "red families" have amassed enormous wealth through their military or political connections and enjoy lives of immense privilege. They attend elite schools and live in walled-in mansions attended by servants and guarded by private security. But it is a precarious life, subject to Beijing's fickle factional currents and occasional tectonic power shifts.

The import of Hunter's arrival with his father on December 4, 2013, was crystal clear to the Chinese when the somber forty-three-year-old descended AF2's stairs behind Joe, to be greeted by a military honor guard waiting on the red carpet below.

This was American power come to do private business.

It wasn't the first time Hunter had met Xi with his father, who had been cultivated by Communist Party leaders since his first visit to China in 1979 as a US senator and later as chairman of the Senate Foreign Relations Committee.

In that role Joe was an early champion of China's entry into the World Trade Organization, a landmark decision that would deal a body blow to America's working class. Millions of manufacturing jobs were lost to cheap Chinese labor, but it was a price US leaders were willing to pay on the expectation that a rising tide of prosperity would lift all boats and that China would join the liberal-democratic world order.

Two decades on, the main beneficiaries of globalization have been the world's richest few, and China, far from liberalizing, has used (mostly American) advances in technology to perfect an unprecedented system of totalitarian repression that Hitler and Stalin could only have dreamed of.

Joe's Chinese connections would unlock doors for his son to the richest sovereign wealth funds and most powerful state-owned enterprises—opportunities that Wall Street titans like Goldman Sachs would kill for.

Hunter had something that money can't buy: the Biden name and, with it, the promise of special access to the top echelons of the American government. Joe lived up to that promise in Beijing, taking time out from his busy schedule to meet with Hunter's new business partner, Jonathan Li (a.k.a. Li Xiangsheng), CEO of the Bank of China-controlled Bohai Capital.

It might have looked odd for a vice president to include members of his extended family in his entourage on state visits, but Joe had long made a practice of it. Along with his son, he brought along the middle of Hunter's three daughters, Finnegan, then aged fifteen, whose presence served to reassure a domestic audience trained to regard Biden family grifting as just good ol' Joe being a family man. The narrative has been honed and repeated for five decades until it is ingrained in America's consciousness.

Few at the time seemed to question the propriety of Hunter monetizing the relationships forged by his father in the foreign countries where Joe was deputized to project American power and prestige.

But even the mildest inquiries about his presence at his father's side on official trips were treated as an affront by Joe. He and his office always swore blind that he knew nothing about his son's overseas business dealings. He simply enjoyed the company of his family while traveling.

The story might have satisfied incurious American journalists. But the Chinese weren't fooled. They understood implicitly the concept of *guanxi*, the Confucian system of personalized social networks and reciprocal obligations that is the foundation stone of Chinese culture going back thousands of years. The chaos of the Cultural Revolution in the 1960s and 1970s only reinforced the importance of guanxi to gaining trust in a country without a tradition of written contracts. Unspoken mutual commitments when doing business in China recognize that family is an extension of the individual.

Guanxi was a way of getting ahead and getting along, which was familiar to Joe from his earliest Delaware days, when he leveraged jobs and other favors for family members from his donors. Everyone knew that when you help Joe's family, "it's just like helping Joe," his Senate staff used to say.

So, even if they didn't speak the same language, President Xi and Vice President Biden understood each other well, from their first official meetings in 2011 when Joe was assigned the task by President Barack Obama of getting to know his enigmatic Chinese counterpart, who was next in line to become supreme leader. Two years later, Xi would greet Joe as "my old friend."

Xi himself was a princeling of sorts. His father, Xi Zhongxun, was a revolutionary hero, Communist Party propaganda chief, and Chairman Mao Zedong's right-hand man. But in 1963, when Xi was ten, his father was purged from the party for "subversion" and paraded in a cone-shaped metal dunce hat by Red Guards, tortured, and jailed. Xi's mother was forced to denounce her husband, and Xi's older sister apparently committed suicide. Xi was forced out of school at age sixteen and sent for reeducation in rural Shaanxi Province, before he and his father were rehabilitated after Mao's death in 1976 under the new paramount leader of the People's Republic of China, Deng Xiaoping.

Xi would ascend to the lofty position in the Communist Party of "core" leader, an honor only ever accorded to Deng and his predecessor Mao. According to family folklore, Xi's father would go on to establish the Shenzhen "special economic zone" under Deng in 1980, as the test site for an export-manufacturing hub bordering Hong Kong to attract foreign investment and launch China's state-led version of quasi-capitalism. During Xi's presidency, his father's role has been accorded greater significance and Deng's role has been diminished.

Xi's life experience thus has informed a hard-nosed view of politics, which he revealed in 2000 in an interview, quoted by the *Wall Street Journal*.

"People who have little contact with power, who are far from it, always see these things as mysterious and novel," Xi said. "But what I see is not just the superficial things: the power, the flowers, the glory, the applause. I see the bullpens [where the Red Guards held prisoners during the Cultural Revolution] and how people can blow hot and cold. I understand politics on a deeper level."

Joe liked to brag that his relationship with Xi was something special. He often claimed to have had "24 to 25 hours of private meetings with him when I was vice president, traveled 17,000 miles with him. I know him pretty well."

You can only imagine what Xi, a chemical engineer by training, thought of the rambling and self-aggrandizing Joe, as relayed in Mandarin by a translator. But the two men had family tragedy in common, neither drank alcohol, and both were proud to have children who were Ivy League graduates: Xi's twenty-nine-year-old daughter, Xi Mingze, attended Harvard. They both were men of modest talent who had risen to the very top.

Over the years, Joe's repeated emphasis on the number of meetings, miles flown, and total hours he had spent with Xi, rather than on the substance of anything achieved, was mystifying to a domestic audience that mistook it for empty boasting. But the metrics reflect a distinctive Chinese sensibility—*wu-lune*—which refers to investment in a long-term relationship between a business and its client.

Joe had pressing assignments to carry out in 2013 on behalf of America and her allies in the region, including persuading China to lay off stealing intellectual property and to stop militarizing islands in disputed waters of the South China Sea, one of the world's most dangerous flashpoints. A week before Joe's visit, China provocatively had imposed an "Air Defense Identification Zone" to control airspace over territory claimed by Japan and South Korea.

But Joe left China empty-handed.

By contrast, the trip was a triumph for Hunter, who walked away with his first big deal in China—the Bohai Harvest Rosemont investment partnership (BHR). It would be consummated on December 16, 2013, twelve days after he flew into Beijing on Air Force Two, when the Chinese business license for the new investment fund was issued by

Shanghai authorities. Hunter officially became a shareholder and member of the BHR board.

Within months, an emboldened China accelerated its reclamation of reefs and atolls around the Spratly and Paracel Islands, constructing a military staging ground with which to control the South China Sea and threaten America's allies.

By January 2019, BHR would have $2.5 billion in funds under management, according to board papers on Hunter's laptop.

As of July 2021, despite saying he would divest himself of his shareholding when his father took office, Hunter still owned a 10 percent share of BHR.

In other words, the son of the US president is in business with the government of Communist China.

During the three days he was in Beijing in December 2013, Hunter "seemed to duck in and out, sometimes joining his father at events and red-carpet arrival ceremonies, and at other times following his own itinerary, presumably with his daughter Finnegan," reported Josh Lederman, an NBC reporter who traveled on Air Force Two with the Bidens.

There is an unusual gap in Hunter's emails between May 2013 and January 2014, and unlike his other trips to China, this one is not marked on his calendar. But we can piece together from other sources what was going on.

We know from Hunter's admission to the *New Yorker* that, shortly after arriving in Beijing, he organized for his father to meet his partner, Jonathan Li, in the lobby of the historic Diaoyutai State Guesthouse, where the Bidens were staying.

The "pool report" from that day, issued by US journalists traveling with the vice president, includes a curious unscheduled interruption: "Vice President Li Yuanchao and Vice President Biden walked into Villa 5 [of the guesthouse] at 12:06 pm and chatted as if they were old chums amongst their staff and friends near the door of the villa and not quite to the point where the official handshake was to occur. Vice President Biden stepped out for four minutes and thirty seconds into a side room, accompanied by security only. Not sure what he was doing. Perhaps an important call."

It is likely that Joe's side room interlude, which delayed his Chinese hosts and the waiting media, was to meet Hunter's partner Li. (A few years later, Joe would write a recommendation letter to Brown University for Li's son Christopher.)

The *New Yorker*'s Adam Entous takes up the story: "According to a Beijing-based BHR representative, Hunter…helped arrange for Li to shake hands with his father in the lobby of the American delegation's hotel. Afterward, Hunter and Li had what both parties described as a social meeting. Hunter told me that he didn't understand why anyone would have been concerned about this. 'How do I go to Beijing, halfway around the world, and not see them for a cup of coffee?'"

However, Entous reports that some of Joe's advisers "were worried that Hunter, by meeting with a business associate during his father's visit, would expose the Vice-President to criticism [over] whether he 'was leveraging access for his benefit.' When I asked members of Biden's staff whether they discussed their concerns with the Vice-President, several of them said that they had been too intimidated to do so. 'Everyone who works for him has been screamed at,' a former adviser told me. Others said that they were wary of hurting his feelings. One business associate told me that Biden, during difficult conversations about his family, 'got deeply melancholy…. It's like you've hurt him terribly.'"

Joe's burden of tragedy again served to insulate him from the criticism that he deserved but also blinded him to the grave risks his family was taking.

During the rest of the visit, Hunter attended just one official engagement with Joe and Finnegan that was recorded by the White House photographer: a traditional tea ceremony, at Liu Xian Guan Teahouse in the Dongcheng District of Beijing, with US Ambassador Gary Locke, and his wife and son.

But Hunter can be seen lurking in the background in another photograph as Joe glad-hands his way through the CCP hierarchy. Before a dinner in the Great Hall of the People, Hunter watched from a short distance as Xi and his father inspected ancient artifacts brought in from the Chinese Museum.

Joe and Xi were reported to have spoken together for an unprecedented 4.5 hours in another room before dinner. It is not known if Hunter had joined them in that "private bilateral," but at dinner Joe emphasized to Xi the importance he placed on personal relationships.

"I believe all politics is personal," said Joe. "Personal relationships are the only vehicle by which you build trust," he told a breakfast of the US-China Business Council the following day. He bragged about the amount of time he and Xi had spent together and declared they were "trying to build a new kind of relationship," one of "mutual benefit."

From the Chinese point of view, the message was clear: I'm your man. Show me you care.

Xi declared at dinner with Joe that the relationship with America would be one of "win win cooperation." But when it comes to China, it's the Bidens, not America, who have done the winning.

Joe knew Xi's economic reforms were a golden opportunity to make money in China and his family would have the inside running.

Xi spent time explaining to Joe the import of the Chinese Communist Party's 18th Congress, which had just ended, having anointed Xi general secretary of the CCP and installing Wang Qishan, Xi's teenage roommate from their forced peasant days in Shaanxi Province, to spearhead the upcoming corruption crackdown that would wipe out his factional enemies.

But Xi wouldn't bother Joe with messy internal politics. He simply told him about the promising economic reforms that had come out of the Congress which would "level the playing field for private and foreign owned businesses," Joe told the breakfast.

He didn't say businesses just like Hunter's, but he didn't need to.

Boasting aside, Joe's ties with China ran deep. He was part of the first delegation of US congressional leaders to visit China and meet leader Deng Xiaoping after the two countries normalized relations in the post-Mao era. Xi, eleven years Joe's junior, was finishing his engineering degree at Tsinghua—China's top university.

Joe was back again in August 2001, his debut leading an overseas delegation as chairman of the Senate Foreign Relations Committee, one month before the Senate vote clearing China's path to the WTO.

President Jiang Zemin invited Joe and his three Senate colleagues for a lengthy charm offensive with Communist Party leaders in the beach resort town of Beidaihe, China's version of Martha's Vineyard.

Joe returned to Washington extolling China's emergence "as a great power, because great powers adhere to international norms in the areas of non-proliferation, human rights and trade," he told the *New York Times*.

By the time Joe returned to China as vice president, in August 2011, Xi was the anointed successor to President Hu Jintao. The two VPs cohosted business dialogues, had long dinners in Beijing, and traveled together to the city of Chengdu, 1,200 miles away in Sichuan Province.

It appears Joe was eager to ingratiate himself with Xi, to such an extent that the *Weekly Standard* was moved to protest with the headline "Biden Embarrasses America, Again."

"Recently, American officials have displayed an unseemly eagerness to please Chinese leaders. Indeed, the vice president's trip risks having the unfortunate feel of a 'tribute' visit to the Middle Kingdom. 'You are our national affairs,' Joe gushed to Xi."

Within six months, Obama had deputized Joe to take the lead on the administration's China policy, originally labeled a "strategic pivot" to Asia and then rebranded a "rebalancing," with the aim of containing the rise of China. A decade later there was not much to show for it, apart from a few more marines stationed in northern Australia.

Weeks after Joe's new role was announced in 2012, Xi made a trip to Washington, DC, and Joe invited Hunter to a luncheon in honor of the Chinese vice president in the Benjamin Franklin Room of the State Department on February 14.

That night Hunter flew to Moscow to meet an oligarch, so he missed the formal dinner Joe held for Xi at his residence at the Naval Observatory.

Xi traveled to Iowa, where he once had stayed in the home of an American family to study US agriculture in 1985. His last stop was Los Angeles, where Joe was waiting to host him for yet another dinner.

While he was in L.A., Xi had a task to perform that would further enhance Hunter's business profile in China. He attended a signing ceremony
for US energy technology start-up GreatPoint, one of Hunter's first clients
for the consulting firm he founded in 2008, Seneca Global Advisors.

GreatPoint Energy had just received a $1.25 billion investment
from Chinese conglomerate Wanxiang Group, the largest foreign venture capital investment into the US that year. Xi was on hand to announce the agreement with his traveling partner, the billionaire owner
of Wanxiang, Lu Guanqiu, and US Commerce Secretary John Bryson.

It is not clear whether Hunter was directly involved in securing
the Wanxiang investment or if Joe was aware of his son's connection to
the ceremony.

But two years later Wanxiang would be involved in another Biden enterprise, buying a distressed electric car company, Fisker Automotive, in
which Hunter had invested through his firm Rosemont Seneca Partners.

Fisker had been granted $528 million in federal loans by the Obama
administration in 2009 to build hybrid electric cars in the Bidens' home
state of Delaware; in fact, in an old factory just four miles from Joe's
house in Greenville. Joe was instrumental in getting federal funds for
the project, Delaware's Chief of Economic Development Alan Levin told
the *Wall Street Journal*. "We had in the vice president a secret weapon,
except there is nothing secret about Joe Biden." A spokeswoman for the
VP told the *Journal* he had made "no direct appeals" to the Department
of Energy. After the loan was approved, at a celebratory breakfast at
his home for United Auto Workers bosses, Joe called the project "a met-
aphor for the rebirth of the country."

By 2013 Fisker had filed for Chapter 11 bankruptcy without building
a single vehicle.

Buried in the list of creditors—which included Leonardo DiCaprio
and Al Gore—reporters found Hunter's name, but could not determine
whether he was an unlucky investor or the owner of a foreign-built Fisker.
Turns out he was both.

Before he hit the big time in China, Hunter bought into every fund-
ing round of Fisker, although how much money he spent is unknown.

"You don't have a problem with highlighting Fisker as an investment, do you?" asked his business partner Eric Schwerin.

In 2013, Hunter used a $7,500 federal tax credit to buy a Finland-built Fisker plug-in luxury sports sedan with woodgrain trim, named a "Karma," but it appears to have been a dog. He traded it in for an imperial blue BMW 740Li worth $80,000 the following year.

After the Chinese bought the company, Hunter received a groveling email from Ni Pin, president of Wanxiang America, and the princeling son-in-law of Xi's L.A. traveling companion, company owner, Lu: "We heard your Fisker was out of order and could not get services. Sorry," wrote Ni. "It would be our honor to get your Fisker fixed."

Hunter replied: "I loved my Fisker but unfortunately due to all the bugs in the system and the loss of service, I sold the car back to the dealer at a big loss."

It may be the only time Hunter came out the loser in a deal with the Chinese. But they soon made it up to him.

CHAPTER

The Super Chairman

"At the top of America's core inner circle of power and influence, we have our old friends."
—Professor Di Dongsheng, Renmin University vice dean of International Studies, November 28, 2020

Who was the mysterious "Super Chairman" who promised to plough $100 million seed capital into Hunter's first big deal in China? Why was his identity such a secret that his American partners referred to him as SC? And why, as Hunter wrote confidentially to his friend and partner Devon Archer, "does the Super Chairman love me so much?"

"It has nothing to do with me and everything to do with my last name," he wrote in a jubilant email on September 23, 2011.

Hunter was cock-a-hoop. He had just pulled off the deal of his lifetime. Or, more accurately, his smooth new partner Jonathan Li, CEO of

Bohai Capital, had engineered a partnership with the Chinese state that Hunter believed would make him very rich, without having to do much more than glad-hand a conga line of powerful bosses, as he had done in Beijing on a quick trip the previous year.

"Keep this between us please," Hunter wrote to Archer. "But bottom line is, if I/you and me get around 7% of this fund it could be in many ways the end all be all [*sic*]. I don't believe in lottery tickets anymore, but I do believe in the Super Chairman.... I know Michael [Lin] can be overly optimistic but if we were 20% owners of a...Super Chairman backed fund, I think the sky's the limit."

Archer replied: "This is smelling more and more real. I do believe in the Super Chairman as well and I [am] starting to believe this is how things actually do go down on the mainland.... Wow."

They had reason to be optimistic. The Bohai Harvest RST (Shanghai) Equity Investment Fund (BHR), in which Hunter would become a director and shareholder, would be backed by Chinese state-owned enterprises worth a combined $8 trillion, including the Bank of China, the Postal Savings Bank, China Life, and the National Council of Social Security.

By 2019, BHR would have $2.5 billion in funds under management. It made acquisitions around the world, from coal mines and dairy farms in Australia to American firms with military technology and artificial intelligence applications, as part of President Xi's imperial Belt and Road Initiative.

The BHR partnership was struck between four parties: On the Chinese side were Bohai, which was controlled by the country's most powerful financial institution, the Bank of China, and another big asset manager, Harvest Fund Management. On the American side were Hunter's Rosemont Seneca and the Boston-based Thornton Group, which joined forces to form Rosemont Seneca Thornton LLC, the "RST" in "Bohai Harvest RST."

Hunter would own 10 percent as one of nine directors of the new US-China joint venture, known as BHR Partners. As his father closed in on the White House, Hunter removed himself as a director of BHR in the fall of 2019, but he still owned 10 percent, through his firm Skaneateles,

LLC, in July 2021, according to China's National Enterprise Credit Information database.

Hunter's lawyer, George Mesires, said in a statement in October 2019 that his client had "committed to invest approximately $420,000 USD to acquire a 10% equity position in BHR" in October 2017 and had received no return on his investment at the time he resigned from the board.

If the stake was of no value, why didn't Hunter relinquish it when he gave up his directorship and sever all ties to a Chinese state-backed investment fund that had already brought so much heat on his father? Hunter was willing to expose his father's reputation to risk at this critical moment and hold on to his 10 percent share because the real payout is yet to come.

The Chinese connection had become too unsavory for John Kerry's stepson. Chris Heinz says he was not involved in the BHR deal and had become so alarmed by this time about the "risks" Hunter and Archer were taking in Ukraine that he was in the final stages of extricating himself from the partnership, said his spokesman Chris Bastardi.

Hunter's partners in the BHR deal had a bigger appetite for risk. He credits Archer—who will later become vice chairman of BHR with an equal 10 percent stake—with the fortuitous daisy chain of introductions that culminated in the deal: "I clearly would never had met SC [Super Chairman] if I hadn't met Jonathan [Li] through Michael [Lin] through Jimmy [Bulger] through you through Chris [Heinz]. Anyway, my point is whatever comes out of this or anything going forward I consider 50/50 between you and me."

Thornton co-founder Jimmy Bulger was the son of former Massachusetts state senate president William Bulger and the namesake nephew of notorious South Boston mob boss James "Whitey" Bulger. Loosely depicted by Jack Nicholson in Martin Scorsese's *The Departed*, Whitey would be beaten to death in prison in 2018.

Although his uncle was convicted of participating in the murder of eleven people, he "was not the monster they made him out to be," Jimmy Bulger says in the documentary *My Name Is Bulger*: "There's a false narrative about my family. We cannot win."

Bulger and Hunter hit it off straight away. "I love Bulger," Hunter writes to Archer. "He writes just like he talks." The affable Bostonian would call Hunter "kingpin" and lavishly praise him after their trips to China where "your presence was a huge boon to us all." He would engineer a meeting in Shanghai in 2016 between Hunter and Alibaba magnate Jack Ma.

Bulger introduced Hunter to his partner, Thornton co-founder Michael Lin, a stocky Beijing-based Taiwan-born former JP Morgan Chase Asia executive, with impeccable connections to high-ranking Chinese and Taiwanese officials.

Lin, fifty-eight, laid out for Hunter what was expected of him by his Chinese partners.

First, make the firm "look internationalized with guolos' [*gweilo*, a gently derisive Cantonese term for Caucasian] faces on the board and ownership structure (of course guolos [we] can trust)."

Second, "Open as many doors as possible in the western world." Third, "Join some of the meetings in Hong Kong and China they arrange when talking to high profile [investors] during the road shows."

It was through Lin that Hunter met Bohai's Jonathan Li, the Chinese businessman who would become the CEO of BHR, and whom Hunter would introduce to his father after jetting into Beijing on Air Force Two in 2013.

Li, in turn, would introduce Hunter to the "Super Chairman."

Four weeks after Joe Biden's first meeting with then-vice president Xi in Beijing, in August 2011, Michael Lin emails Hunter and Bulger with the good news that a deal with Bohai is in the works: "All right, Gents, let me give you a heads up of my meeting with [Bohai's] Jonathan [Li] last night. Nice to have such a great and longtime buddy!

"A PE [private equity] Fund; 2% annual management fee. Carried: 20%. Fund I size: USD300 million. Fund I will have a RMB fund and a USD fund with a size of USD150 million, respectively."

Lin tells them he has a $100 million commitment from the Super Chairman and goes on to quote their as-yet-unnamed benefactor.

"Super Chairman went: 'I'm not being greedy even though I commit US$100 million. Actually, I'm planning to give part of the remaining 70% to other Chinese big firms which I'm going to invite to join us, companies like China Investment Corp. or that kind of high-power companies.'"

Lin explains: "This is surprisingly great for us. Companies like CIC and the like will of course even enhance [our fund's] profile and credibility and to make the fund pie even much bigger.... Imagine we will be sitting on the same board with CIC or the other Chinese HUGE investment fund house(s)!!!"

In another email Lin describes how ownership of the fund would be divided among the partners. The Super Chairman gets 40 percent, Jonathan Li and his team get 30 percent, "and we three 30 percent (Isn't this nice and sweet?!)"

The following day Lin emails the "cooperation term sheet"—a "strictly confidential" preliminary template for a legal contract—spelling out the precise terms for the deal. It would be set up to deliver management fees worth 2 percent of the funds under management, minus expenses, to its partners.

The expected life of the fund would be eight years, with a potential two-year extension. The profit, or "carried interest," when the investments are harvested at the end of the life cycle of the fund, is to be allocated in an 80-20 split, with 20 percent to be shared among the "General Partners," which includes Hunter. It is unknown whether the same terms survived the fund's evolution to BHR.

But the Term Sheet does reveal, for the first time, the identity of the "Super Chairman."

There are four "General Partners" listed on the term sheet: Hunter is "Party B," Lin and Bulger are "Party C," and "Management Team" is "Party D."

"Party A" is Ever Union Capital, a firm incorporated in the tax haven of the British Virgin Islands, according to the "Paradise Papers" investigation by the International Consortium of Investigative Journalists.

The sole director and stockholder of Ever Union Capital is forty-one-year-old tycoon Che Feng (or Fung in Cantonese), the son-in-law of high-ranking CCP member, Dai Xianglong.

This was the Super Chairman. Che was one of more than a dozen Chinese princelings found to be using offshore companies in the British Virgin Islands, according to the "Paradise Papers," including President Xi's own brother-in-law, Deng Jiagui, a real-estate developer.

A Bloomberg investigation in 2012 found more than $1 billion in assets, including luxury properties in Hong Kong, had been amassed by Xi's siblings. While Bloomberg connected no assets directly to Xi, the story quoted Roderick MacFarquhar, a Harvard expert on Chinese elite politics, about the crucial advantage in business enjoyed by relatives of powerful figures in China.

"Automatically people will see you as a potential agent of influence and will treat you well in the hope of gaining guanxi [connections] with the bigwig relative."

It is hardly surprising that the Chinese would perceive the same advantages for themselves in the US when doing business with the son of an American vice president; it would be naïve for Americans not to appreciate the expectations attached to Hunter Biden's shareholding in a Chinese firm, inclusion on a Chinese board, and access to the inner sanctum of China's elite.

But Super Chairman Che's connection to Hunter would not save him from what followed. He would become a victim of a "corruption" crackdown as President Xi consolidated his power.

Xi's anti-corruption drive has widely been seen as cover for a political purge, targeting rival factions—especially members of the "Shanghai Gang," associated with former president Jiang Zemin and allied "red families."

The Shanghai Gang's opposition to Xi's increasingly dictatorial leadership intensified in 2018 when he abolished the two-term limit for president and vice president, which had been put in place in the 1980s to prevent a Mao-like tyrant reemerging.

The move cleared the way for Xi to remain in power for life. In case the point was lost on anyone, he appeared at a celebration of the 100th anniversary of the CCP in the summer of 2021 dressed as Chairman Mao. Xi appointed his closest ally, Wang Qishan, to head his corruption purge and then made him vice president in 2018.

Super Chairman Che was caught in Wang's corruption net through his alliance with Ma Jian, the powerful vice minister at the Ministry of State Security—China's equivalent of the CIA and FBI combined.

The spy chief was convicted of corruption and sentenced to life imprisonment in 2018. Both Ma and Che reportedly were part of the "Shanghai gang." According to a Chinese language article from Radio France International, Che was "suspected of acting as Ma Jian's thug."

To add to this web of intrigue, one of Ma's closest allies was fugitive New York billionaire Miles Guo—a.k.a. Guo Wengui, a.k.a. Miles Kwok, a.k.a. Guo Haoyun—an associate of former Trump adviser and China hawk Steve Bannon. Guo also was a major investor in Super Chairman Che's special effects firm Digital Domain, which worked on one of the X-Men blockbusters.

Guo fled China in late 2014 and, soon after arriving in the US, bought a $68 million penthouse overlooking New York's Central Park and joined Donald Trump's private Mar-a-Lago Club in Florida.

For a Chinese dissident, Guo struck a curiously insouciant figure, giving interviews to the Western media and posing for photographs in the splendor of his new surrounds.

His Chinese-language GTV Media Group would run lurid material from Hunter's laptop after the *New York Post* broke the story in October 2020. But some Chinese-language websites also made false claims about the material, feeding a perception that the story was disinformation and that respectable news organizations were right to ignore it.

Guo's attacks on the Xi regime made him a high-value enemy of the CCP. According to a Trump insider, Xi's first request of Trump over dinner at Mar-a-Lago in 2017 was to extradite Guo.

In 2018, Guo accused Xi's corruption tsar Wang Qishan of having an affair with the Chinese movie star Fan Bingbing. After the allegations were aired, Fan, the most famous woman in China, was arrested for tax evasion and disappeared for months.

Wang, like Xi, is a princeling, the son-in-law of the former vice premier responsible for the brutal crackdown on the 1989 Tiananmen Square protests.

He also happens to be the chief contact in China for Wall Street elites.

At the height of the Trump trade war in September 2018, Wang, newly elevated by Xi to be his vice president, summoned senior Wall Street executives to Beijing to figure out how to persuade the White House to back down.

Stephen Schwarzman, head of The Blackstone Group, was there, along with big wigs from firms such as Goldman Sachs and Morgan Stanley, reported the *New York Times*. Frustrations about the Trump administration's approach to China were aired by both sides. It was a stark contrast to the situation in the late 1990s when Wall Street titans successfully leaned on President Clinton to support China's entry into the World Trade Organization.

Wang Qishan told his American visitors that Beijing was offering Wall Street lucrative opportunities to expand in China, if only the administration would be reasonable.

But Donald Trump, who had dubbed himself "Tariff Man," wouldn't listen.

In the words of Beijing professor Di Dongsheng, an intimate of President Xi, "Wall Street couldn't fix Trump."

Di, the vice dean of International Studies at Renmin University, made an extraordinarily candid televised appearance in front of a live audience in Shanghai three weeks after the 2020 US presidential election, describing a secret network of "old friends" that had penetrated the highest levels of government and Wall Street.

He named Hunter, whose business deals he claimed had been facilitated by the CCP to advance its own interests.

"For the past 30, 40 years we have been utilizing the core power of the United States.... Wall Street had a very strong influence on the domestic and foreign affairs of the United States. So, we had a channel to rely on....

"Why, between 1992 and 2016, did China and the US, used to be able to settle all kinds of issues? No matter what kind of crises we encountered…things were solved in no time [because] at the top of America's core inner circle of power and influence, we have our old friends."

But Donald Trump's election in 2016 had disrupted this cozy relationship.

"During the US-China trade war, they [Wall Street] tried to help, and I know that my friends on the US side told me that they tried to help [but] Wall Street couldn't fix Trump."

With comical glee, Di said: "But now we're seeing Biden was elected," and the audience erupted in laughter.

"Trump has been saying that Biden's son has some sort of global foundation. Have you noticed that?

"Who helped him build the foundations? Got it?

"At such a time, we use an appropriate way to express some goodwill…. If we understand this matter from the perspective of the international political economy, I think there is a tactical and political value in it."

Deng's candor reflected a growing arrogance among China's elites toward the United States.

The soaring trade deficit with China over the previous two decades had transferred the wealth of America's middle class to China's "red families" and bankrolled a global buying spree geared around its national ambitions.

During the period from 2010, when Hunter and his family were doing business with the CCP, Chinese foreign direct investment in the US grew from less than $1 billion annually to nearly $5 billion in 2010, reaching a peak of $45 billion in 2016, according to the Rhodium Group.

After the election of Donald Trump, annual investment dropped sharply, hitting $29 billion in 2017, collapsing to $5.4 billion in 2018, before rising slightly to $7.2 billion in 2020. The Bidens' tiny home state of Delaware was one of the top states targeted for Chinese investment, behind California and Pennsylvania.

The fact that Chinese corporate leaders received covert government subsidies and loans meant they were able to make investments in the US with none of the normal expectations for return on capital. "This allows [the] Chinese to invest in deals that benefit U.S. political leaders, their families or allies in anticipation of a quid-pro-quo on future policies impacting China or Chinese investments," cybersecurity expert Jeff Johnson told the U.S.-China Economic and Security Review Commission in 2017.

Investment in the US by the Chinese government and its proxies was "our 21st Century opium," he warned.

———————•◦•◦•◦———————

Super Chairman Che has not been seen since he was detained for questioning in Beijing in June 2015.

Hong Kong newspaper *Oriental Daily* reported he was found guilty of money laundering and transferring illegal proceeds to foreign countries. He also was accused of selling intelligence to Western intelligence agencies, an offense punishable by death.

But at his first recorded meeting with Hunter, in April 2011, in Beijing, Che was master of his universe. He hosted a lavish dinner for the vice president's son at his private club, Courtyard in the Air, atop the striking dragon-head-shaped skyscraper Pangu Plaza, Hunter's diary shows. The $1 billion building was owned by Che's sometime business partner Miles Guo, from whom it was confiscated after he fled for New York.

Che had "high-end clubs in Beijing and Hong Kong, using beautiful women to serve high-ranking officials and rich people of all kinds," reported the *Epoch Times*, an anti-Beijing newspaper backed by the outlawed religious movement, Falun Gong.

Hunter and his American partners apparently enjoyed themselves.

"Thanks for the great time last week—we had a blast with you and Super Chairman Che in Beijing!" Bulger wrote to Jonathan Li on his return to the US on April 28, 2011.

Hunter followed up the next day: "Jonathan, You are the best. I was so glad to see you in good spirits and good health. I am in full agreement with Jim—between all of our organizations we should be able to achieve a great deal. Just give me my marching orders."

Thornton's Lin replied to all: "Che is pleased to get us engaged in this deal [and] Jonathan will soon help come up with the deal intro/info and let us know the cooperation mechanism among us."

"Nicely done savage beast!" replied Bulger. "We are standing at attention over here waiting to leap into action."

Che's courting of Hunter had begun at least fifteen months earlier through Li, whose first appearance on the laptop is a condolence email oozing an unctuous familiarity with the Biden family.

"Please accept my sincere condolences [for the loss of] dear grandma Mrs Jean Biden," Li wrote on January 22, 2010, after the death of Joe's mother at age 92. "I know how much she meant to you and your family... so many people join you and your family in sorrow...our thoughts are with you and your family at this sad time."

Within a few weeks Li had organized Hunter's first trip to Beijing, Secret Service detail in tow. Archer, Bulger, and Lin joined him for three days of meetings with China's most powerful state financial institutions—which collectively manage almost $2 trillion and are controlled by the Chinese government. Some would become investors in BHR.

In Beijing on April 7, 2010, Hunter's diary shows a meeting with Ji Guoqiang, general director of equity management at the National Council for Social Security, a state-owned enterprise with $120 billion of assets under management. Over the next two days he had meetings with: Lei Zhang, founder of Hillhouse Capital, a private equity firm with $50 billion under management; executives of $1 trillion sovereign wealth fund CIC and China Life Asset Management, the largest asset manager in China, with more than $400 billion in assets under management; executives from the Postal Savings Bank of China; and lunch with Xin Wei, chairman of the Peking University Founder Group, a state-owned technology conglomerate connected to high-ranking CCP officials.

It was extraordinary access to the inner sanctum of China's financial elite for a fledgling firm run by a neophyte with no knowledge of the country.

In later years Devon Archer will claim that the BHR partnership came about after he met Jonathan Li in a cigar bar in Manhattan in 2012. But the laptop shows that Li's involvement with Hunter had started at least two years earlier.

The importance placed on Hunter's family connections was highlighted in a press release on the Thornton website trumpeting his April 2010 trip, in which he was featured prominently as "the second son of the US Vice President Joe Biden."

In a later meeting with the president of the Taiwan-based Fubon Financial, Hunter "offered to send an autographed Joe Biden book" to an executive, emails show. (Joe's books are a standard business gift from Hunter and his partners, concrete evidence of their powerful connection to the US government.)

After his successful first trip to Beijing, Hunter flew back to Washington, DC, just as Chinese President Hu Jintao was arriving for the 2010 Nuclear Security Summit. Joe met Hu, but there is no indication that Hunter did.

His diary shows he was five miles across town on April 11, attending Sunday brunch at the home of millionaire philanthropist Adrienne Arsht, who used to lend her Mediterranean-style palazzo on Biscayne Bay in Miami to his dad and Jill. The 1913 Villa Serena once had been the winter home of the three-time presidential candidate William Jennings Bryant, so perhaps Joe drew inspiration there for his multiple runs at the White House.

By September of the following year Hunter tells Archer in an email: "We need to talk about super chairman fund. Things are moving rapidly and the percentage he is offering me is much larger than I at first thought."

Archer replies: "This can be a serious opportunity. Not only on its own merits from an economics standpoint but from the leverage in access it provides with the big boys here in the west who all need China; from Tiger to Blackstone to Carlyle etc."

In October, six months after his first meeting in Beijing with the Super Chairman, Hunter would fly to meet Che again in Hong Kong, with his Secret Service detail.

The highlight of Hunter's two days in Hong Kong was another dinner party Che threw in his honor on Thursday night, October 20, 2011, in his private club atop the Citicorp Centre in Causeway Bay with spectacular views across Victoria Harbour.

Hunter wrote to Jonathan Li the following week to thank him for "facilitating the meeting in Hong Kong last week. I know I speak for Jimmy and Michael as well, we are grateful for your including us in this exciting endeavor and we are fully committed to making this a roaring success with you at the helm."

After all this time, Archer was still in the dark about the identity of their benefactor, sending an email to Hunter: "What's Super Chairman's actual name?"

"Mr Che," replied Hunter.

Super Chairman Che disappears from the laptop after that trip, as mysteriously as he appeared. There is no evidence that his business relationship with Hunter continued. But Jonathan Li would continue working with Rosemont Seneca Thornton on the fund that would become BHR.

He would secure approval for the US-China joint venture with his "boss," Yue Yi, then executive vice president of the Bank of China.

A few weeks after Hunter's return from his final visit with Che in Beijing, the US media was full of stories about Joe's new leading role in the Obama administration's "next phase China policy."

The *New York Times* ran a headline: "Biden May Take On Expanded Role in Foreign Policy in Second Term: Vice President Joseph R. Biden Jr.'s stature is likely to rise with the departure of other foreign-policy heavyweights."

Hunter forwarded the story to Archer with the comment: "If we can't figure this out, we should be shot."

CHAPTER

Show Me the Money

"My son has not made money from China."
—Joe Biden, October 2020, final presidential debate, Nashville

There really wasn't a lot for Hunter to figure out. China was offering itself on a plate to the vice president's son. He even worked it so that he wouldn't have to put up any cash for his 10 percent share of BHR.

Jonathan Li, BHR's CEO, had promised "we will get help in form of loan or otherwise to meet obligation," Hunter wrote to Archer on May 7, 2014. "I made it clear in no uncertain terms that we do not have the capacity to find [cash] now w/o guarantee of income from fund in the immediate. OK?"

Sure enough, three years later, $158,000 was wired to Hunter from BHR, on December 3, 2017, labeled "registered capital payments." Eric Schwerin, his Rosemont Seneca business partner, reminds him in an email: "This is the money that Jonathan is loaning to each of the US shareholders so that they can pay the remaining amount of their registered capital. The loan will be paid back from any distributions made. I think this was actually your suggestion to Jonathan awhile back as a way to avoid having to come up with more cash from the US shareholders."

What exactly his new Chinese state partners thought they were paying for is not spelled out on the laptop, but the ease with which BHR's acquisitions in the US passed scrutiny raises questions about the regulatory environment at a time of record Chinese investment.

When he flew into Beijing on Air Force 2 with his father in 2013, there was little media interest in Hunter's business dealings in China. But in July 2014, the *Wall Street Journal* started snooping into BHR.

A series of panicked emails by Archer ensued.

Lindsay Wright, Harvest Global Investments Limited CEO in Hong Kong, emails Hunter, Archer, and Bulger on July 7, 2014, with a "heads up" about the *WSJ* inquiries. Wright has told the paper that BHR is a joint venture "between Bohai, Harvest Group and Rosemont, Seneca Thornton and Team [with a] focus on cross border M&A [in] high end manufacturing, consumer, financials and energy (principally gas)."

Archer isn't happy with the description.

"If the *WSJ* calls back," he emails Wright, "I would ensure you qualify that the BHR JV is with Hunter and I as individuals. How we were advised by counsel was to do it this way and I just want it to be clear. I don't think it's a big issue but wanted to make sure that's how it's presented: 'Hunter and Devon, whose firm is Rosemont Seneca, but the JV is with us as individual private citizens.' Thanks."

Later on it will become clearer why they're so adamant about this apparently minor detail.

The next day Archer pings Wright again: "This reporter has been calling around many colleagues and partners of Hunter and me overnight…. Anything that gets into the news cycle seems to mushroom with false speculations."

Wright replies that the questions are "pretty generic so it is somewhat a factual piece, as I see it, nothing more than that."

Archer: "Oh good. That makes me feel better."

It's not apparent why Hunter and Archer want to be listed as private citizens in the joint venture, but Jonathan Li intervenes with an email to Archer saying the attempt won't fly.

"I think to put it as your individual investment may not work. BHR registration with Shanghai free trade zone [is] stated as Rosemont Seneca. This document can be accessed by the reporters."

On July 9, Wright emails from Hong Kong: "Finished the questions with WSJ this morning…. As outlined by Jonathan I DID NOT clarify with them that your investment is personal and not Rosemont, Seneca and Thornton Group. Only advised this is American Group COLLECTIVELY owning 30%.

"They also queried whether our industry focus in resources was linked to Hunter being on board of Ukraine gas—I advised NOT LINKED."

The next day Li emails the group: "Article is very good." Panic averted.

On legal advice at about the same time, Hunter, Archer, and Bulger began the process of splitting their joint 30 percent stake in BHR, which was held by Rosemont Seneca Thornton, LLC, a firm incorporated in Delaware on May 28, 2013, as a consortium of Hunter and Archer's Rosemont Seneca Partners and Bulger's Thornton Group to facilitate their joint venture with the Chinese.

Bulger would first remove his 10 percent share of BHR, leaving Hunter and Archer to place their remaining 20 percent stake in a new entity, Rosemont Seneca Bohai, LLC, a firm incorporated in Delaware on September 18, 2014, with Archer as director. (Rosemont Seneca Bohai also received monthly director payments from Burisma for Hunter and Archer totaling $166,666 until February 12, 2016, after which Hunter's half started being paid to his firm Owasco.)

In an email on October 2, 2014, BHR's Felix Yu told the board the ownership changes were being done "for the purpose of tax efficiency" and described the process as a "registration amendment" with Chinese regulators.

"As advised by outside counsel, Rosemont Seneca Thornton LLC, as one of the shareholders of [BHR], should transfer to Rosemont Seneca

Bohai LLC its 20% equity interest in the Company and to Thornton Group its 10% equity interest." It would take until June 24, 2015, for the equity change to be formalized.

All this maneuvering would take on greater significance in 2020, when the Grassley-Johnson Senate report stated that Hunter was paid $3.5 million in 2014 by Elena Baturina, the wife of the corrupt former mayor of Moscow. The allegation was based on a wire transfer to Rosemont Seneca Thornton, dated February 14, 2014, which showed up in a "suspicious activity report" submitted by the bank to the Treasury Department.

Hunter's lawyer George Mesires denies that Hunter profited from the transaction, telling CNN: "Hunter Biden had no interest in and was not a co-founder of Rosemont Seneca Thornton, so the claim that he was paid $3.5 million is false."

At the time that Baturina allegedly wired $3.5 million to Rosemont Seneca Thornton, Hunter and Archer's joint 20 percent share in BHR also was being held by the firm. The process of transferring their equity out of the firm would not begin for another eight months.

The question of who pocketed the Russian millions has never been answered.

But Hunter undoubtedly had an association of some sort with Baturina. He and Archer had a meeting with her at the Villa d'Este, a haunt of Russian oligarchs overlooking Lake Como, Italy, on April 4, 2014, seven weeks after the alleged wire transfer.

Baturina also featured in emails that month between Archer and Hunter about a potential real estate deal in Chelsea, New York, and a Latin American cocoa venture.

A year later, Baturina and her husband, Yury Luzhkov, would appear on a guest list Hunter prepared for a dinner with his father at Washington's Cafe Milano.

Because Rosemont Seneca Thornton is incorporated in "business-friendly" Delaware, there is no visibility into its ownership. Its registered agent is listed as VCorp Services, a company whose service provides anonymity to beneficial owners of companies.

According to the Delaware Division of Operations, Rosemont Seneca Thornton was canceled as a business entity on June 1, 2017, for "Failure to Pay Tax" of $1,770.

But well before this unfortunate event, in December 2014, Hunter and Archer began another convoluted process to split their joint 20 percent BHR shareholding.

Half was transferred to Archer's firm Ulysses and the other half to Hunter's firm Skaneateles.

"It is important for RSB [Rosemont Seneca Bohai] and Skaneateles to document their mutual understanding on the transfer price payment ie no cash change hands will happen," writes Cloris Mao, a lawyer acting for Hunter from Mesires's firm, Faegre Drinker Biddle & Reath, to "Gilbert" Xiaochuan Han of BHR on December 9, 2014.

Gilbert replies that any payment arrangement between Hunter and Archer should be "set out in a side agreement among parties instead of admitting it to the regulators."

Mao replies: "I have moved the RMB 3 Million ($460,000) payment language to a side agreement."

Eighteen months later there is yet more upheaval, when Archer is arrested and charged with securities fraud and has to remove himself from the BHR board.

Hunter is dragged into the case, as Mesires fields a series of questions from the US Attorney's Office about his role in Burnham Asset Management and his relationship with Archer and co-defendant Bevan Cooney.

Mesires writes to Archer's lawyer on June 8, 2016, wanting to "use the opportunity to strip out Hunter's 10 percent interest which I understand has been fully funded (or very close thereto) and is to come from [Rosemont Seneca Bohai's] holdings."

On August 10, 2016, Mesires spells out how he sees Hunter's role.

"We view RSB as acting as Hunter's agent in holding funds that RSB has accumulated on Hunter's behalf from various third party payments to Hunter (eg Burisma).... To effectuate the equity transfer, Hunter is directing that RSB transfer its 10% interest in BHR to Skaneateles."

On March 10, 2017, seven weeks after Joe leaves office, Schwerin emails Hunter and Mesires: "Paperwork to conclude the transfer of the 10% shares of RSB to Skaneateles. Also, Devon is transferring his shares to [wife] Krista."

Hunter will remain in business with the Chinese Communist Party through his father's campaign and into his presidency. He appears determined to keep his share of BHR until he can reap the spoils. He clearly has judged those spoils to be valuable enough to risk damaging Joe's presidency.

So, let's take a closer look at BHR. Its stated objective was investment in new and emerging technologies, artificial intelligence, and robotics. But many early acquisitions were standard Belt and Road initiatives, including mines and farms.

This accorded with China's Five-Year Plan of 2011, which targeted cross-border investments in food companies, agriculture, seeds, and agri-chemicals. Chinese investment in the agricultural sector grew tenfold in less than a decade. In 2013, a Chinese conglomerate bought the world's largest pork producer, American company Smithfield Foods.

BHR's 2015 acquisition of Henniges Automotive, a Michigan car parts maker of anti-vibration technologies with military applications, turned out to be its most controversial investment.

The $600 million buyout of Henniges by BHR and state-owned aircraft company Aviation Industry Corporation of China was one of the biggest takeovers in history of an American automotive firm by a Chinese company.

Because Henniges's technology had potential national security implications, the deal needed special approval from the Committee of Foreign Investment in the US (CFIUS), of which a key member was Secretary of State John Kerry, Archer's former boss.

In the contacts file on his laptop, Hunter listed the direct number of someone at the "CFIUS office" at the US Department of Commerce. The person could not be found, so the name has not been included here. But concerns over the opaque CFIUS review process that existed at a time of record Chinese investment in the US would lead in 2018 to the enactment of the Foreign Investment Risk Review Modernization Act.

Potential conflicts of interest involved in the Henniges automotive deal drew the attention of Republican Senators Grassley and Johnson.

Their Senate inquiry into Hunter's overseas business dealings was kicked off by Grassley's letter in August 2019 to the Department of Treasury requesting documents related to the Henniges sale's CFIUS approval and "any potential coordination with the Obama-Biden White House."

The senators later would complain that their inquiry's access to relevant documents and testimony was "persistently hampered by criminal investigations, impeachment proceedings, COVID-19, and several instances of obstructive behavior." House Democrats, in turn, claimed the inquiry was a "Russian disinformation campaign."

The Henniges transaction was the first of BHR's US deals, and the company's 2015 Christmas newsletter described it as a "momentous milestone."

In confidential BHR board papers on the laptop, dated January 17, 2019, Henniges is listed as having increased revenue by 11.4 percent to $760 million for the first three quarters of 2018, while profits had declined.

In 2014, BHR invested in Sinopec, the Chinese state-owned refinery giant, taking a 1.7 percent stake of SMC, the retail arm that runs its chain of 60,000 gas stations and convenience stores.

In 2017, BHR invested $30 million in Face++, a facial recognition firm whose technology has been linked to Beijing's mass surveillance of Uighur Muslims. The 2019 board papers say Face++ "is currently valued at USD 4 billion" and BHR's shareholding was 1.88 percent, so the investment had more than doubled.

BHR also held US$25 million of bonds in Australia's Watagan Mining, a subsidiary of Yancoal, and had facilitated the 2017 sale of Brownes Dairy in Western Australia to an onshore Chinese fund.

The papers showed that the fund had accumulated assets under management of RMB 16.4 billion ($2.5 billion) as of January 2019 and had set up fourteen shell funds in the tax haven of the Cayman Islands.

In 2017, operating profits were disappointing, at about $300,000 on revenue of $14.2 million.

The advent of the Trump administration had hurt business: "2018 was an extremely difficult year," the board papers say. "The China-US trade conflict has caused the United States and European countries to strictly restrict China from investing and making mergers and acquisitions of high-tech and advanced manufacturing companies."

The forecast for 2019 "remains bleak" the papers warned, although operating profit was expected to rise to RMB 26 million ($4 million).

Heinz had counseled his partners, Hunter and Archer—both of whom he described as "naïve"—not to expect quick profits from private equity, but their emails show a growing disillusionment with BHR.

"We all want to get cash back from BHR," wrote Mike Leonard, Thornton's vice president of operations, in an email to Hunter and Bulger on August 25, 2016.

"That was the ultimate goal when undertaking this endeavor. That being said, we recognize it takes time to grow a business, close deals and make successful exits. However, the other night Jonathan [Li] made clear that we won't be seeing any dividends for at least the next two years....

"Will Henniges potentially generate a carry of $10 million to be split among the partners or will it generate $100 million?... There needs to be more discussion on how the partners get their cash back."

Schwerin was trying to extricate himself from the mess at Rosemont Seneca in March 2019 when he reminded Hunter and his lawyer Mesires about the $158,000 loan from Jonathan Li: "There is a high likelihood that that there will be a distribution [from BHR] in 2019 that would repay that loan and still provide a distribution to Skaneateles."

He also declared that there will be lucrative "future distributions" to BHR from companies bought, including Henniges, Sinopec, and Face++. "All of these investments are likely to be profitable for BHR."

If Schwerin is correct—and the soaring value of Face++ suggests he is—this means that Hunter is set to make a significant profit at the end of the fund's life, which could be any time from 2022. To avoid political controversy, he presumably would wait until his father is out of office to crystalize any profits.

By the time Hunter's BHR shareholding was transferred into his private company, in March 2017, Hunter had divorced Kathleen, and his relationship with his sister-in-law Hallie had become fodder for the gossip pages.

He also had embarked on a more promising Chinese venture with energy conglomerate CEFC, the capitalist arm of President Xi's Belt and Road Initiative. This time Uncle Jim will be beside him to ensure he gets the cash he needs.

CHAPTER

The Big Guy

*"I've seen Vice President Biden saying he never talked to Hunter
about his business. I've seen firsthand that that's not true."*
—Tony Bobulinski, October 22, 2020

Hunter and his Uncle Jim were already waiting for Tony Bobulinski in the lobby bar of the Beverly Hilton when he arrived at 10:00 p.m. on May 2, 2017.

The Bidens had chosen a discreet couch behind a thick marble column where they could see everyone who walked in the front entrance. Joe Biden was flying into Los Angeles to speak at the prestigious Milken Institute Global Conference and would be joining them at the bar within the hour.

For Bobulinski, forty-eight, a third-generation Navy veteran and Democrat donor, it would be his first meeting with the recently retired vice president, and he was conscious that he was being vetted for a trusted role orchestrating the Biden family's existing joint venture with Chinese energy conglomerate CEFC.

"Dad not in now until 11," Hunter wrote in a WhatsApp message. "Let's me [you] and Jim meet at 10 at Beverly Hilton where he's staying."

When Bobulinski arrived at the bar, Uncle Jim, seven years younger than his brother and more heavyset but still a dead ringer for Joe, greeted him like an old friend, although it was the first time they'd met.

At that hour the only other person in the bar was casino operator Steve Wynn, sitting with a woman on the other side of the room.

Hunter and Bobulinski drank water while Jim ordered a club sandwich with fries and explained that the meeting with Joe was strictly "high level."

"We will not go into any detail about the business," said Hunter. "I just want my dad to be comfortable with you."

At 10:38 p.m., Joe arrived through the hotel's front entrance with his Secret Service entourage, and Hunter jumped up to intercept him. Five minutes later he brought his father to the table.

Bobulinski stood up to shake Joe's hand. "This is Tony, Dad," said Hunter, "the individual I told you about that's helping us with the business that we're working on with the Chinese."

Joe began by talking about the Biden family, their tragedies, and his political career. Bobulinski described his background as a wrestling champion on a scholarship at Penn State and briefly outlined an impressive résumé, including as a nuclear engineer and instructor in the Navy's elite Nuclear Power Training Command with a high-level security clearance.

"Thank you for your service," said Joe. "Thank you for helping my son."

Jim and Hunter told Joe that Bobulinski had been "working hard" on the Chinese deal and Joe said: "My son and my brother trust you emphatically, so I trust you."

Bobulinski had passed the test. It was a crucial meeting, because for the first time an outsider would see the extent to which Joe was involved in Hunter and Jim's international business. Joe was the final decision-maker. Nothing important was done without his agreement.

The conversation wrapped up within forty-five minutes. Joe was tired, but he invited Bobulinski to meet him again at 8:30 a.m. the next day in the hotel ballroom to hear him speak at the Milken confab of chief executives, wealthy investors, and fund managers.

As soon as he got home, Bobulinski messaged Jim Biden on WhatsApp at 11.40 p.m.: "Great to meet u and spend some time together, please thank Joe for his time was great to talk thx."

The next morning, May 3, 2017, Bobulinski went back to the Beverly Hilton and sat at the head table listening to Joe talk on stage with L.A. billionaire and notorious insider trader Michael Milken.

Backstage afterwards, Joe asked: "What did you think of my speech?" They walked outside together to his waiting car and shook hands.

"Keep an eye on my son and brother and look out for my family," Joe told him.

Bobulinski then headed across Santa Monica Boulevard to the Peninsula Hotel to meet Jim, who was sitting alone in a blue and white cabana by the rooftop pool on a glorious sunny day.

For two hours he was regaled with Biden family folklore, going back to Joe's first Senate election in Delaware in 1972, when Jim, twenty-three, dabbling in the nightclub business after dropping out of the University of Delaware, became his brother's chief fundraiser. Jim filled him in on the efforts he and Hunter had made for CEFC the past two years, leveraging Joe's name to advance the CCP's Belt and Road agenda around the world.

As Jim talked, Bobulinski marveled at the political risk to Joe's career if his family's flagrant influence peddling during his vice presidency came to light.

"How are you guys getting away with this?" he finally asked. "Aren't you concerned that you're going to put your brother's [2020] presidential campaign at risk? You know, the Chinese, the stuff that you guys have been doing already in 2015 and 2016, around the world?"

Jim chuckled and looked knowingly at Bobulinski. "Plausible deniability," he said, using a term of art coined by the CIA during the

Kennedy administration to describe the practice of keeping the president uninformed about illegal or unsavory activity so he can plausibly deny he knows anything if it becomes public knowledge.

Bobulinski understood Jim meant that Joe knew what his family was doing in his name but was insulated from the dirty details. It was why Jim and Hunter had instructed Bobulinski the previous night to keep the business talk with Joe at a vague "high level".

Occasionally they would let their guard down, but the family was "paranoid" about keeping Joe's involvement quiet, Bobulinski would be told.

He soon learned to decode the euphemisms related to Joe, which made him a dangerous foe three years later when he became so disgusted that he blew the whistle on the shady enterprise.

"I've seen Vice President Biden saying he never talked to Hunter about his business," Bobulinski would say in a bombshell statement to the *New York Post*'s Michael Goodwin on October 22, 2020, a few days after the paper began publishing material from Hunter's laptop. "I've seen first-hand that that's not true, because it wasn't just Hunter's business. They said they were putting the Biden family name and its legacy on the line....

"I don't have a political ax to grind; I just saw behind the Biden curtain, and I grew concerned with what I saw. The Biden family aggressively leveraged the Biden family name to make millions of dollars from foreign entities even though some were from communist controlled China."

But the disillusionment was to come later.

————•◆◆•————

The Bidens started wooing Bobulinski in 2015 through a mutual friend, James Gilliar, a wiry, fifty-six-year-old British ex-SAS officer based in the Czech Republic, where he had come to know Ye Jianming, the forty-year-old spendthrift chairman of CEFC.

Chairman Ye's task at that time was to spend $1.5 billion as quickly as possible to ensure the Czech Republic would become China's "Gateway to the European Union," a priority of President Xi.

To that end, Ye bought everything from a football team and a brewery to an airline, before being named "special economic advisor" to Czech President Milos Zeman.

Now he was looking for an influential partner to help with Belt and Road acquisitions in other locations around the world that had strategic significance for the Chinese state.

Gilliar, nicknamed "MI5" by Bobulinski, after the British spy agency, connected with Hunter through trusted Biden family friend Rob Walker, a former Clinton administration official whose wife, Betsy Massey Walker, had been Jill Biden's assistant when she was Second Lady.

Gilliar emailed Walker in February 2015 to praise Hunter's appearance in Beijing at a board meeting of the fledgling fund BHR.

"Hunter was great," Gilliar wrote to Walker. "True sheikh of Washington."

He emailed Hunter a few weeks later: "It has been made clear to me that CEFC wish to engage in further business relations with our group."

Gilliar knew CEFC was the capitalist arm of President Xi's Belt and Road Initiative to spread China's influence—and debt traps—across the world. No Chinese company executed its goals more ardently than CEFC and its young chairman, who was dubbed the "Belt and Road billionaire" in the press.

Chairman Ye had built his provincial energy company into a Fortune 500 colossus virtually overnight, an achievement described by Chinese news agency Caixin as "another great enigma in the miraculous world of Chinese business." He enjoyed the support of President Xi and had ties to the PLA, as former deputy secretary general of its propaganda arm, the China Association for International Friendly Contacts (CAIFC).

In a rare interview with Caixin at CEFC's palatial marble headquarters in Shanghai's upscale French Concession District, Ye is portrayed as a "hermit king" sitting on a golden chair in "a room that resembles a miniature Great Hall of the People."

Uniformed staff members wearing earpieces glide by. "Most of them were young women wearing smart clothes and bright faces." Ye's face was "as expressionless as a stone statue. Amidst the gilded surroundings, his canvas shoes had an eye-catching plainness....

"In his public activities as a private entrepreneur, Ye Jianming is always walking alongside important foreign political figures. He has been photographed with world leaders such as Israeli President Peres, Turkish President Erdogan, Chadian President Déby, and European Commission President Juncker. He has met with the Crown Prince of Abu Dhabi, and the Prime Minister of Bulgaria held a feast to welcome him."

In the winter of 2015, Chairman Ye and his offsider, CEFC Executive Director Jianjun Zang, a.k.a. "Director Zang," flew to Washington, DC.

A meeting with Ye was scheduled in Hunter's diary for December 7, 2015, in a week that was a swirl of back-to-back Christmas parties hosted by Joe and Jill at the vice president's residence at the Naval Observatory.

One of his former associates, who spoke on condition of anonymity, believes that Hunter brought Chairman Ye to meet Joe at one of those parties. There is no indication of any such meeting on the laptop, but Hunter had a pattern of introducing business associates to Joe when they came to DC, and a holiday party would have been an effortless way for him to impress his wealthy Chinese partner and casually introduce him to his father.

"Dinner with CEFC" was scheduled into Hunter's diary on Thursday, August 11, 2016, at Cafe Milano in Georgetown, an Italian restaurant where he entertained foreign clients in a private room. His father came to at least one such dinner while vice president. But Joe was vacationing in the Hamptons with Jill in August 2016, so it is unlikely he attended Hunter's CEFC dinner.

After a frustrating experience in another Chinese deal as a minority partner in private equity firm BHR, in which the payday would not come until the end of the fund's life, Hunter and Jim wanted more control of the CEFC partnership and a regular income stream.

This is where Bobulinski fits in. A naval nuclear commander turned wealthy institutional investor, he came highly recommended by Gilliar to build what they planned would be a world-class investment firm, called SinoHawk.

The two men had an easy camaraderie born of a shared military background and ten years crossing paths in their globe-trotting careers.

In December 2015, Gilliar tells Bobulinski he needs help structuring a Chinese joint venture for "one of the most prominent families in the United States."

The plan is to "build an investment firm like Goldman Sachs," he writes in the WhatsApp message.

"The family is the Biden family," Gilliar will soon disclose. Joe, who has announced that he will not run for president in 2016, will be actively involved once he leaves office, and the Bidens expect billions of dollars of projects to flow through the company, Gilliar says.

He lets Bobulinski in on the last piece of the puzzle in March 2016: the Bidens' Chinese partner is CEFC, which has "more money than God," he writes. "This is the capital arm of one belt one road."

At about this time, Bobulinski is introduced to Rob Walker, who tells him he is "a proxy for Hunter Biden, Jim Biden and the Bidens around the world."

Finally, in February 2017, Gilliar sends Bobulinski a WhatsApp message saying he wants to introduce him to his "partner."

"Who is your partner?" asks Bobulinski.

"Hunter Biden," replies Gilliar.

Bobulinski is leery. "I understand you want me to…help drive things in the US, but Hunter is [already] here."

Gilliar: "Money there, intent there…skill sets missing…. We need to create the best deal platform in history, and they haven't got a clue."

Bobulinski doesn't like the fact Hunter "was kicked out of US Navy for cocaine use."

"But he's super smart," says Gilliar. "Just a lot of under achievers around them using their name. Has a few demons but u are used to those, right?"

Bobulinski asks: "Is he the decision maker or the Chinese?"

Gilliar: "New platform. Best discuss face to face but I'm the driver."

Later, Bobulinski asks: "Ok who is putting up the $10MM [million]?"

Gilliar: "Joint vehicle—half us and then equally split—money is already in. Discuss more face to face."

On March 5, Page Six breaks the news that Hunter and his brother's widow Hallie are an item.

When Hunter doesn't show up for a scheduled meeting three days later in New York, Gilliar tells Bobulinski it doesn't matter: "In brand he's imperative but right now he's not essential for adding input to business."

It is at this point that Gilliar explains to Bobulinski that the Chinese involved in CEFC are "intelligence so they understand the value added" of the Biden name.

Bobulinski remains troubled by Hunter's scandals, and Gilliar, who is in Australia with Director Zang looking for acquisitions in March, is worried he might pull out. So, he arranges for him to meet Hunter the following month at the Chateau Marmont, in Bobulinski's hometown of L.A.

They meet by the hotel pool in April and speak for two hours while Hunter chain-smokes. Bobulinski finds him respectful and polite. Hunter boasts that he has his father's ear and can bypass his advisers.

"I want Dad to meet you," Hunter says.

Hunter tells Bobulinski how the joint venture vehicle should be structured and expresses caution about US laws, including the Foreign Corrupt Practices Act (FCPA), which prohibits businesses paying bribes to foreign officials. He appears to conflate that law with the Foreign Agents Registration Act (FARA), a 1938 antispying law that requires anyone acting as a lobbyist for a foreign power to register with the US government as a foreign agent.

"No matter what, it will need to be a US company at some level in order for us to make bids on federal and state funded projects," Hunter writes.

"Also, we don't want to have to register as foreign agents under the FCPA which is much more expansive than people who should know choose not to know."

"Regardless we should have a…company called CEFC America, and ownership should be 50 me 50 them. We then cut up our 50 [percent] in a separate entity between the 4 of us."

Hunter seems focused, but Bobulinski is puzzled about Uncle Jim's frequent meddling in CEFC business.

For instance, in April Jim pulls strings at New York's elite Horace Mann School to get Director Zang's daughter Rouqi fast-tracked for entry, although she ends up enrolling in another school.

Jim also writes a letter on behalf of CEFC to New York Governor Andrew Cuomo requesting a meeting. "We intend to discuss potential projects and investments in New York." He lists the other attendees as Hunter, Chairman Ye, Director Zang, and an unnamed "Member of the Royal Family of Luxembourg."

"What is the deal w Jim Biden as he wasn't part of the discussion but now seems a focal point?" Bobulinski asks Gilliar. "What role does Jim see himself playing?"

"Consultant is what he's offered as [far as] I know," Gilliar replies. "He [Hunter] brought in Jim simply to leverage getting more equity for himself and family in the final hour, that is evident."

In another WhatsApp message, Gilliar tells Bobulinski: "With H [Hunter's] demons, could be good to have a backup, he [Jim] strengthens our USP [unique selling point] to Chinese as it looks like a truly family business, and I like the dude."

A big part of Jim's role was to keep Hunter out of trouble, something he would fail at miserably the following year. Like Hunter, Jim, his wife, Sara, and daughter Caroline lived beyond their means. Their insatiable need for cash at times became an intolerable burden for Hunter.

Less than two weeks after meeting Joe Biden in Beverly Hills, Bobulinski incorporates SinoHawk Holdings LLC, on May 15, 2017, having decided against Hunter's suggestion they call it CEFC America. It will be a global investment firm seeded with $10 million of Chinese money that will buy projects in the US and around the world "in global and/or domestic infrastructure, energy, financial services and other strategic sectors," says the contract he has drawn up.

SinoHawk would be 50 percent owned by Ye, through a Delaware-incorporated CEFC entity, Hudson West IV LLC. The other 50 percent would be owned by Oneida Holdings LLC, another Delaware firm set up by Bobulinski.

Oneida would be split according to an email sent by Gilliar to the group on May 13, 2017, laying out the distribution of shares.

Ten percent of the company would be allocated to Joe Biden.

"The equity will be distributed as follows," wrote Gilliar, listing the shares in percentages.

"20 H [Hunter]

"20 RW [Walker]

"20 JG [Gilliar] "20 TB [Bobulinski] "10 Jim [Biden] "10 held by H for the big guy."

Three years later, Bobulinski will tell the world that "there is no question" that the "big guy" is Joe Biden. "Hunter Biden called his dad 'the Big Guy' or 'my Chairman,' and frequently referenced asking him for his sign-off or advice on various potential deals that we were discussing."

Joe was called "the big guy" in other emails on Hunter's laptop or in WhatsApp messages on Bobulinski's phones. In one case, a Serbian associate of Hunter's, Vuk Jeremić, past president of the UN General Assembly, who was on a $330,000 retainer from CEFC, refers to Joe as "big man."

Gilliar warned Bobulinski, in a WhatsApp message on May 20, about the need for discretion about Joe's role: "Don't mention Joe being involved, it's only when u are face to face, I know u know that but they are paranoid."

Bobulinski, already frustrated by Hunter's demands, replied: "OK they should be paranoid about things."

Three weeks after his father left office, in 2017, Hunter flew to Miami with Gilliar and Walker to meet Chairman Ye, who was there for the Miami International Boat Show.

They booked into the $700 a night beachfront Nobu Hotel on Monday, February 13, 2017, and scheduled lunch with the Chinese for Thursday in a private room set for ten at the Bourbon Steak restaurant in the ritzy JW Marriott Turnberry Resort & Spa, where Ye was staying with his entourage.

But Hunter flew home the day before the lunch. He already had met with Ye, over a private dinner on the Tuesday night, at which the CEFC chairman made him an offer too good to refuse: $10 million a year, for a minimum of three years, for "introductions alone," as Hunter would later assert in an imperious email to CEFC executives. Unbeknownst to Bobulinski and Gilliar, SinoHawk was dead.

Ye sealed the new alliance with a rich gift—a 3.16 carat diamond. Photographs of the stunning stone appear on Hunter's laptop along with a grading report that lists it as a "round brilliant" of Grade F with prime "VS2" clarity and "excellent" cut.

The gift could not have come at a better time. Hunter was in the middle of an ugly divorce from Kathleen, and his office manager, Joan Peugh, had just sent him the latest in a series of overdue bills, a tax collection notice from the District of Columbia for $47,226.78.

Hunter would tell the *New Yorker*'s Adam Entous that he had flown to Miami to meet Chairman Ye purely for charitable purposes, hoping to secure a donation to World Food Program USA, the nonprofit on whose board he served and which he had used before as a cover for his foreign business activities.

Hunter said it was just chance that the altruistic encounter "turned to business opportunities" and claimed to be surprised when Ye gave him the diamond. He didn't mention the happy coincidence that his business partners Gilliar and Walker were with him in Miami to clinch a business deal with CEFC.

Nor did he mention the astonishing $30 million dollar sweetheart deal he had struck with Ye the night the diamond materialized.

Hunter told Entous he gave the diamond "to his associates and doesn't know what they did with it." It never occurred to him that the diamond was a bribe. "What would they be bribing me for? My dad wasn't in office."

But the diamond was just an appetizer.

Nine days after Hunter's meeting in Miami with Ye, $3 million is wired into an account for Rob Walker's company, Robinson Walker LLC, from State Energy HK Limited, a Shanghai-based company linked to CEFC, according to the Grassley-Johnson inquiry.

On March 1, another $3 million is wired to Robinson Walker by the same company. Both transactions are flagged by the Department of Treasury's Financial Crimes Enforcement network in a "suspicious activity report," filed with the Senate committees as "Confidential Document 16."

Using the document as a source, the Grassley-Johnson report of November 18, 2020, says: "At the time of the transfers, State Energy HK Limited was affiliated with CEFC China Energy, which was under the leadership of Ye Jianming. In the past, State Energy HK Limited transferred funds to at least one company associated with Hunter Biden's business associate, Gongwen Dong....

"These transactions are a direct link between Walker and the communist Chinese government and, because of his close association with Hunter Biden, yet another tie between Hunter Biden's financial arrangements and the communist Chinese government."

Further tying Walker to the $6 million transactions from CEFC is a WhatsApp message on May 21, 2017, he sent to Bobulinski in which he confirms that he is the owner of Robinson Walker: "I have an llc: Robinson walker llc."

The Senate report concludes it is "unclear what the true purpose is behind these transactions [$6 million from CEFC] and who the ultimate beneficiary is."

We know from the laptop that Hunter received regular payments from Robinson Walker. One document lists $56,603.74 from Robinson Walker as income for Rosemont Seneca Advisors, between June and December 2017.

Rob Walker paid at least $511,000 to Hunter's firm Owasco in 2017, according to an email from Hunter's tax accountant, Bill Morgan.

Payments to Hunter from Robinson Walker are referenced again in an email titled "2016 Tax Docs" from Eric Schwerin to Hunter's lawyer Mancinelli on February 16, 2017: "Hunter does not receive [tax forms] 1099s or W2s from Burisma or Robinson Walker but those numbers are reflected in the [Hunter's law firm] Owasco W2 and P&L [Profit & Loss]."

Walker tells Bobulinski his role in CEFC is "being a surrogate for H [Hunter] or Jim when gauging opportunities, i.e. digging around in Texas on high speed rail with some of my republican friends...or hitting new countries and contacts abroad where things are lukewarm, but not hot enough for H to close or too odd for H to be present...

"Been doing this with James for a bit already and it seems to work well. Places in Africa, such as Angola, where James [Gilliar] and I have been planning to go to for a bit to take a look at forestry/timber operation...would be a good idea for me to go w/James and show an American face that has the political knowledge and BS that may not be time spent wisely for H or Jim."

Angola, one of the world's poorest and most corrupt countries, has had its valuable forests plundered by illegal logging by Chinese companies.

Through 2015 and 2016, Hunter and his partners had been using the Biden name to open doors for CEFC around the world, in Kazakhstan, Georgia, Oman, Ukraine, Romania, and beyond.

Now that Joe was out of office it was time to be paid.

In an email on April 18, 2017, written by CEFC project manager Cui "Caesar" Can, to Gilliar, the Chinese expressed their appreciation for the "B [Biden] family" and suggested a meeting with Chairman Ye.

"Please convey...greetings to the B family, their support is the base of CEFC's further development.

"Director Zang and Chairman Ye will visit the US together in May, they are willing to have a meeting with H and you by any chance. Will discuss further cooperation opportunities in the US/Middle East/Europe then."

The meeting in New York will prove explosive.

16

Limestone Jesus

"I'm the only one putting an entire family legacy on the line."
**—Hunter Biden WhatsApp message to
Tony Bobulinski, May 18, 2017**

Hunter was enraged and pounding the table, eyes bulging. "You owe my family $20 million!" he screamed at CEFC Director Zang Jianjun, the high-ranking CCP official who sat impassively across the table from him.

"We've done work for you all over the world the last couple of years. Why haven't we been paid?"

Flanked by an entourage of bodyguards and interpreters, Zang eyed the angry American until he ran out of steam, and then tactfully navigated the conversation back onto the joint venture contract they were there to sign—the consummation of a two-year agreement with the Biden family.

Within months, Zang will be meeting personally with Vladimir Putin, negotiating China's biggest investment in Russia, on behalf of President Xi. CEFC will be at the center of a seismic shift in Sino-Russian relations with profound national security implications for the United States.

But, for now, at a midtown Manhattan restaurant that Sunday, May 7, 2017, he had to endure Hunter's tantrum.

Sitting alongside Hunter, his American partners squirmed.

"If H pulls another stunt like Sunday lunch it will be difficult," James Gilliar messaged Tony Bobulinski the next day.

Hunter had been on edge since arriving in New York with Uncle Jim in tow. They were there to ink a deal two years in the making with Chinese energy conglomerate CEFC, which they expected would make them all very rich.

The joint venture, SinoHawk, gave them an equal partnership with a company that had rocketed into the Fortune Global 500 with annual revenues exceeding $30 billion. CEFC was the capitalist arm of President Xi Jinping's imperialist Belt and Road Initiative to export Chinese influence around the world.

But, to Hunter's consternation, at the last minute, CEFC's enigmatic forty-year-old chairman, Ye Jianming, who had been cultivating him assiduously for almost two years, was a no-show for their Sunday meeting.

In his place, Ye had sent the serenely plump Zang, forty-two, who served as CEFC's executive director and who, as a CCP official, had the dual role of keeping an eye on the chairman, whose lavish taste and Western affectations were a provocation to some party officials.

Hunter felt disrespected and desperate. His income had dried up since his father's term as vice president had ended four months earlier. His monthly Romanian checks had stopped altogether, and his monthly Ukrainian installments, which had reliably brought in $83,333 a month for three years, had been cut in half. His first Chinese deal, a 10 percent cut of the private equity fund BHR, wasn't delivering the ready cash he needed to fund his lifestyle and meet his heavy family obligations.

His divorce from Kathleen had lumbered him with $37,000 a month in alimony. His addictions were weighing him down, and his fights with his sister-in-law turned lover Hallie had become achingly similar to the ones he had endured with Kathleen.

Everything depended on finalizing this joint venture with Chairman Ye, and the son of a bitch hadn't bothered showing up.

Two days earlier, it was pouring rain when Bobulinski, Gilliar, and Walker checked into the Refinery Hotel near Bryant Park, a chic former hat factory, which boasted the best rooftop bar in the city. The meeting with CEFC to sign the deal was set for Sunday, but there was no sign of Hunter or his uncle Jim.

"Ping H so he feels involved," Gilliar wrote Bobulinski in a WhatsApp message. "He's a delicate flower."

"Jesus," Bobulinski replied. "I don't want to babysit."

At this point, the two men believed Hunter's father—freshly freed of the constraints of high office and central to the joint venture with the Chinese—would join them.

"Think Joe may come Sunday. I'm hoping," Gilliar messaged Bobulinski on WhatsApp.

"Yah, I told Jim that's a no brainer," he replied. "If he can make it he should be here."

If Joe couldn't make it, they had a backup plan.

"Jim trying to get mayor [Bill de Blasio] to come or maybe [billionaire former mayor Michael] Bloomberg," Gilliar wrote.

It was a twenty-minute walk up Madison Avenue to the Four Seasons, where Ye was staying with his wife and entourage who had flown in from Shanghai on his $35 million Gulfstream G550 corporate jet.

But Ye's most pressing business that weekend was not the Bidens. He was meeting executives of the New York–based brokerage firm Cowen Inc. to pay $100 million for a 19.9 percent stake in their bank. The acquisition later would run into problems with the Committee of Foreign Investment in the US [CFIUS] and collapse.

But at the time, a giddy Ye boasted to the Chinese news agency Caixin: "This purchase is second only to Morgan Stanley."

It was his wife's birthday, and Ye had booked the ballroom of the Four Seasons for a party.

He also had to do the final inspection of his new penthouse at 15 Central Park West, on the fortieth floor of the building dubbed the "Limestone Jesus" and billed as the "World's Most Powerful Address," in Michael Gross' book *House of Outrageous Fortune*.

Ye paid $50 million cash for the ex-Barclay Chief Executive Bob Diamond's 5,300-square-foot apartment. Panoramic views over Central Park and the Hudson River made the building a favorite with oligarchs who had money to burn.

It was in the penthouse's vast chef's kitchen where Ye would personally cook lunch for Hunter that summer.

Always on the prowl for a dollar, Jim Biden tried to get in on this juicy Manhattan real estate action. He walked CEFC's Director Zang around the Upper East Side looking at luxury pads in the hope of getting a cut of the agent's commission.

In April, Uncle Jim struck a deal with a real estate broker from Nest Seekers International to split the commission for the sale of Manhattan's last intact Gilded Age mansion and direct the cash to his daughter Caroline. The six-story townhouse at 854 Fifth Avenue had once belonged to the granddaughter of the railroad baron Cornelius Vanderbilt and was on sale for $50 million.

"I will share the commission in the sale of an apartment to your wealthy Chinese client who lives currently in Shanghai," wrote real estate broker Ryan Serhant—the star of Bravo's reality television series, *Million Dollar Listing New York*.

The April 12 email to Jim continued: "So you're aware, commissions are paid to Nest Seekers and I get 70% of that amount...so Caroline would receive 50% of the 70%."

Unfortunately for Caroline, the sale didn't go through.

Director Zang is about to have visa problems, and he and his family will be blocked from entering the country, an indication of trouble ahead.

In June, Ye would outlay another $33 million in cash on a 4,030-square-foot apartment on the eighty-sixth floor of 432 Park Avenue.

Ye wasn't the only tycoon paying top dollar for foreign assets. A reverse gold rush was underway in China to push money into the West before President Xi's next purge.

When he first emerged in America, seemingly from nowhere, the young Shanghai billionaire instantly gained entrée into the highest echelons of New York society, a privilege money alone can't buy.

Plenty of foreign oligarchs have tried and failed to crack elite Manhattan. But doors were opened for Ye by the mysterious socialite Angela Chen, alleged by the Senate Committee for Homeland Security to have links to Chinese military intelligence through her chairmanship of the China Arts Foundation, founded by Deng Rong, the daughter of Supreme Leader Deng Xiaoping.

A board member of the exclusive Philharmonic-Symphony Society of New York, cochair of the Philharmonic's International Advisory Board, and a luminary of the Leonard Bernstein Circle, the forty-something Chen was a fixture at the Lincoln Center in the 2010s.

She glided around Avery Fisher Hall in an elegant red sleeveless Zang Toi evening gown embroidered with musical motifs at the Chinese New Year Gala. She dazzled in red-sequined Armani with Henry Kissinger on opening nights at the New York Ballet.

It was a one-block totter in her Louboutins from the American Friends of the Louvre party with I. M. Pei at the Four Seasons to her Upper East Side abode, Ivanka and Jared's old apartment in the Trump Park Avenue building—which she bought in 2017 for $16 million cash.

Chen was invited to high society dinner parties at Ghislaine Maxwell's garishly decorated $15 million townhouse. She threw dinner parties of her own with a chef flown in from China making Deng Rong's favorite Shanghai dishes for such luminaries as Trump's Secretary of Commerce Wilbur Ross.

Chen introduced Ye to her elite circle, and soon enough he, too, was swanning around the Lincoln Center, appearing in the social pages with Kissinger and Alan Greenspan, the long-term former Federal Reserve chair.

Ye quickly absorbed the social pieties of his new milieu, establishing a nonprofit think tank named the China Energy Fund Committee, which was devoted to climate change and "business ethics." He appointed the gregarious eye surgeon and former Hong Kong Home Affairs secretary Patrick Ho to lead it, and they sprinkled around generous annual grants for "sustainable energy technologies leadership and innovation."

CEFC named itself one of the "Top Ten Chinese Philanthropic Enterprises" four years running, and in 2011 the United Nations granted it "special consultative status" for its philanthropy, an honor that would lead, ultimately, to Ye's downfall.

By 2017, Ye had moved his wife, Wu Liqiong; daughter Yiken Ye; mother, Rongyu Qiu; and nanny, Lizhen Yao, to Manhattan on B1/B2 visitor visas. His son, Junkun Ye, already was in New York on an F1 student visa, attending the exclusive Columbia Prep, on the Upper West Side, where Barron Trump, the then-ten-year-old son of Donald and Melania Trump, was a student. Ye's mother-in-law and chef remained in Shanghai.

With Hunter's help, Ye would apply for visas in September for the rest of his household in preparation for a new life in America, where he planned to go into partnership with the Biden family in the US subsidiary of CEFC.

To that end, Hunter made preparations for his father, uncle Jim, and "my partner" Ye to share his office space in Washington, DC. He ordered new keys and a nameplate to attach to the door of his $17,000 a month corner suite in the House of Sweden building on the Georgetown waterfront. A showpiece of modern Scandinavian design housing the embassies of Sweden and Iceland, the futuristic building was all Swedish maple and glass walls with panoramic views of the Potomac River and the Watergate complex. It also was conveniently just half a mile from a favorite Biden family haunt, Cafe Milano.

The Biden Foundation was the nonprofit Joe launched when he left office in 2017.

Hudson West III was a company incorporated in Delaware by CEFC in April 2016, which Hunter and Jim had started using in August for their own Chinese deals, unbeknownst to Bobulinski and partners, who still were operating under the assumption that SinoHawk was about to be funded by CEFC to the tune of $10 million.

Hunter and Uncle Jim had other ideas. In March 2018, ownership of Hudson West III (HW3) would be legally assigned to Hunter's firm Owasco and Coldharbour Capital, the company co-owned by Chairman Ye's lieutenant Mervyn Yan, according to emails between Yan and Hunter's lawyer George Mesires. Although Yan is a co-owner of Coldharbour Capital, the business address associated with the firm is the same as the home address listed in phone records for his colleague Gongwen "Kevin" Dong in Great Neck, New York.

The six-bedroom house at that address is in a bucolic part of Long Island bordering Manhasset Bay and features a tennis court and pool. Built in the style of a French chateau, it features a vast marble entry hall with Grecian columns and baroque chandeliers. It was sold in 2014 for $6.7 million, according to Zillow, and was back on the market in January 2021 for $6.2 million.

While ownership of Hudson West III was split evenly between Hunter's firm Owasco and Yan's Coldharbour, the capital contribution of $5 million came only from the latter. Owasco contributed nothing, according to the HW3 agreement dated August 5, 2017, and signed by Hunter and Yan.

The agreement also specified a monthly salary for Hunter of $100,000, plus "business expenses" up to $50,000 a month, while Jim would draw $65,000. (HW3 would be dissolved later in November 2018, according to a "Certificate of Cancellation" from the State of Delaware.)

"Please have keys made available for new office mates Joe Biden, Jill Biden, Jim Biden, Gongwen Dong, Chairman Ye CEFC emissary," Hunter wrote to House of Sweden General Manager Cecilia Browning on September 21, 2017.

"I would like the office sign to reflect the following:

"The Biden Foundation

"Hudson West (CEFC US).

"The lease will remain under my company's name Rosemont Seneca.

"If you need information on the individuals above, please refer to their wiki pages.

"Chairman Ye, my partner: Ye Jianming (Chinese…born June 5, 1977 in Pucheng, Fujian) is Chairman and Executive Director of CEFC China Energy Company Limited, a Global Fortune 500 energy and finance conglomerate. He is also Chairman of China Energy Fund Committee, a Hong Kong-based think tank with consultative status with the UN, Chairman of the Academy of Chinese Culture, Director of the Shanghai Energy Security Research Center, Chairman of CEFC Shanghai Charity Fund, Economic Adviser to President of the Czech Republic, and Political Adviser to the New People's Party of Hong Kong."

Also in the email, Hunter included a link from New York real estate publication *The Real Deal* to prove Dong's bona fides as a tenant who could afford the rent.

"Why buy one trophy apartment when you can have two?" ran the headline.

"Hong Kong financial executive Gongwen Dong just shelled out $33 million for a condominium at 432 Park Avenue—just three months after buying a penthouse at 15 Central Park West for $50 million."

In fact, while Dong signed the deeds, the trophy apartments were for Chairman Ye, and he wasn't done yet.

In December 2017, Ye signed a contract to pay a record $80 million for a 20,000-square-foot townhouse with a red-velvet movie theater and its own panic room at 12 East 69th Street.

The deal fell through, along with the Biden family partnership with CEFC, when Ye went missing in Shanghai in February 2018, after being detained by Chinese authorities on the direct orders of President Xi, according to the *South China Morning Post*.

But that unpleasantness still lay ahead.

———— •••• ————

Hunter is in an agitated state when he finally arrives in New York the night before the contract signing with CEFC's Director Zang. He and Uncle Jim find Bobulinski and Walker in the Refinery's rooftop bar.

Gilliar has gone to the Four Seasons to show Zang the contracts.

"U on way back?" Bobulinski messages Gilliar on WhatsApp on May 6, 2017. "H is fired up over something.... Rob Jim and I r on the roof... any clarity on where mtg is tmrw?"

Gilliar replies that he is on his way back with the good news that Zang "didn't change anything except adjust the language around the 5MM [million] loan and 10 MM."

"Sure, but it's an LLC so it's only to allow them to get money out of China and it's non-recourse," Bobulinski replies.

The "framework agreement to establish a joint venture with CEFC" Bobulinski has drawn up for Sunday's meeting is between CEFC and the Biden firm, with CEFC putting up all the cash.

"The issued share capital of the JV shall be US$10,000,000 divided into 1000 shares with each of the Shareholders holding 50 per cent of the shares," reads the contract.

"Subject to a mutually agreed loan agreement, Party A [CEFC] agrees to make available to Party B [Oneida] a loan of US$5,000,000 which shall be used exclusively for the payment of Party B's capital contribution...."

"The main business of the JV shall be to provide consulting services in global infrastructure, energy and other strategic sectors for Party A and/or its Affiliates."

Hunter will be executive vice chairman of the SinoHawk board, and Bobulinski will be chief executive officer, with the Chinese taking the other two board positions as chairman and chief finance officer.

An accompanying document prepared for the meeting trumpets the Biden team's contacts in countries where "prestige has been established": Colombia, Luxembourg, Oman, Romania. It says that they already have "engaged in-country contacts" in Argentina, Belgium, France, Mexico, and the United Arab Emirates.

Hunter and his team bring to the table a "strong and easily definable relationship between our key U.S. executive(s) and their relations in the target country with the following persons: a. senior political figures; b. royal family and/or aristocracy if they exist; c. dominant commercial/

business figures and/or oligarchs." These contacts create "rapid market entry" for deal flow.

Another document titled "Key domestic contacts for phase one target projects" includes Democratic luminaries from around the country, including New York Governor Andrew Cuomo and Senators Chuck Schumer and Kirsten Gillibrand. California Senators Dianne Feinstein and Kamala Harris are listed and then-San Francisco mayor Gavin Newsom is described as "Hunter's friend."

Also cited are "foreign friends" who can be tapped for Belt and Road development projects. They include Colombia's president, Juan Manuel Santos; Argentina's president, Mauricio Macri; Ireland's taoiseach (prime minister), Enda Kenny; and the richest man in India, Mukesh Ambani.

Mexican billionaire Carlos Slim is listed as "very friendly."

Despite Hunter's histrionics with Director Zang at the restaurant, in the end, both men signed the SinoHawk contract, as Bobulinski confirmed in an email to CEFC's Shanghai headquarters that afternoon.

That night, Hunter blows off steam at a strip club. His Platinum American Express card shows a $3,530 charge at Vivid Cabaret a block from the Refinery Hotel.

Hallie is expecting him home: "Where are you?" she texts. "On train? Call me please?? Instead of yelling."

Hunter replies: "You are ridiculous. No more Hallie gets to be as spoiled and selfish as she wants while expecting everyone to bend to her needs. Get a fucking grip. You are cold. I am trying to fucking save my entire professional life and I shouldn't leave here until the Chinese do but instead I'm feeling guilty for missing the 7th train."

Hallie: "Are you on train? I guess not on train. So then stay till you need to and then head to DC and see your kids. Don't come to see me and make me feel bad. I love you but I don't want to pull you away from things you want to do."

Hunter: "Great idea Hallie. I'll start to do what I want to do. Please honey you're sick and I get it but it's not my fault and it's also not my fault that I need to work."

Pressure is piling on Hunter from all directions. His partner and best friend Devon Archer is being prosecuted on federal fraud charges over a $60 million scheme to rip off one of the poorest Indian tribes in America, the Oglala Sioux.

The US attorney has just issued subpoenas for his Rosemont Seneca emails, which inevitably will involve Hunter.

"The government and Devon are in dispute concerning the review of the documents, especially concerning potentially attorney-client communications," Hunter's lawyer, George Mesires, emails him on May 17, 2017.

"As discussed, Devon has included your name as a search term to use to identify potentially attorney-client communications. Devon is suggesting that because you are a lawyer you could have potentially rendered legal advice and he could assert attorney-client communications."

Archer is doing his best to protect his friend.

As if life wasn't complicated enough, Kathleen is pestering him about unpaid bills.

"You are HILARIOUS!!" she writes on May 21, a month after their divorce. "Our credit is a mess because of you. I am trying to get the bills in order—it's been a little difficult because you haven't helped. Many of these accounts are in your name and I can't access. You have completely ruined your own credit and mine—YOU.

"Also, are you ever going to pay your bills? Pay my parents back? The lawyer? The accountant?... You are a joke. You can't stop talking to the girls about money—how you're broke because you gave me all the money—laughable. You are broke but you and your girlfriend are looking at houses in DC?

"Your drama is exhausting—your lying, your addiction, your sick relationship.... Every comment I get from you is a joke—you can't hurt me anymore because I have no feelings for you—except exhaustion and sometimes pity. You are as sick as anyone I've ever met—nothing left of the man I was married to for 22 years."

Despite Hunter's dramas, the CEFC joint venture SinoHawk has been moving ahead.

Gilliar writes an email to Hunter, Bobulinski, and Walker on May 13 with the subject line "Expectations," and includes details of "remuneration packages" for the six partners.

Hunter will be paid an annual salary of $850,000 plus "office expectations."

Bobulinski will also receive $850,000, Gilliar $500,000 plus $15,000 per month travel expenses, and Walker $500,000.

Jim Biden's salary is listed as "unknown."

Gilliar will continue with "international development" for SinoHawk in Oman, France, Belgium, Luxembourg, Azerbaijan, and Colombia, plus "we have found a UAE [United Arab Emirates] bank they want."

But Hunter is not happy. He gripes that $850,000 a year is nowhere near enough to make ends meet.

On May 16, he replies to Gilliar: "I will need a hell of a lot more than 850 p/y on a monthly basis. And this is my own personal problem, but I'll make it yours also I'm sure (Ha)—$2M to me means $1M before taxes. The other half goes to her [Kathleen]—850 to me means 100K to me—she has a 750 floor. That does not include all the debt I assumed and not one dime for the girls (two Ivy league school living expenses and the most expensive high school in DC)."

Bobulinski replies: "H—we have to pay a team of people who will be working 100 hours a week so we generate enough profits so we are distributing $10s of MM [millions] out to the owners."

The next day Hunter is snippy with Bobulinski: "TONY that is what Zang implied—they are both coming to be MY partner, to be partners with the Bidens. He has implied that the #1 has made that clear and available to him."

Recipients of the message understood that "#1" was President Xi. This is the code Hunter used when he referred to the Chinese leader.

In other words, Hunter is making the extraordinary claim that President Xi has taken a personal interest in the CEFC partnership with the Biden family.

Hunter uses the bombshell to try to leverage more cash.

"Come on man," Hunter messages Bobulinski. "We both want the same thing…. Just happens that in this instance only one player holds the trump card and that's me. May not be fair but it's the reality because I'm the only one putting an entire family legacy on the line and if you think it's reasonable that I turn the keys over to someone that I've spent less than 12 hours with then that makes me nervous. So I'm asking you to do us all a favor and find a different way to alleviate your worries."

Bobulinski messages Gilliar privately, to express frustration at Hunter's demands: "We need to manage Hunter as every discussion makes me feel like he thinks things are going to be his personal piggy bank….

"I don't want to be getting a call from H [Hunter] demanding we distribute daily weekly nonsense because he can't manage his life. That's his problem for sure. I don't want an accounting nightmare. And the JV is only distributing cash annually."

Gilliar replies: "Tony, I ain't that stupid. Know why Ye wants the deal and what makes it enormous. It's the family name in reality. They could have asked for 51 percent, maybe u would not be interested but many US moguls would have been."

Bobulinski: "Man, I get that. We just need a good rationale…. You need to stress to H, does he want to be the reason or factor that blows up his dad's campaign. Things need to be done right and [be] protective of that fact."

"Man U are right—let's get the company set up, then tell H and family the high stakes and get Joe involved," Gilliar writes.

Bobulinski messages Gilliar later: "I talked to H and have lawyers thinking about blind trusts for him or other precautions."

As CEO of SinoHawk and managing member of Oneida, Bobulinski has a fiduciary obligation to ensure the company is properly run.

At this point he has no idea Hunter is a crack addict, but after the New York tantrum with Director Zang, Bobulinski determined to structure Oneida to give himself three of seven voting shares on the board, while Hunter, Uncle Jim, Walker, and Gilliar have one each. This would ensure that the "Biden bloc"—Hunter, his uncle, and family friend Walker—didn't control the board.

Hunter hates the idea.

On May 19 he tells Bobulinski in a WhatsApp group chat that his father, "My Chairman," has rejected the corporate structure.

"Hey TONY, I have an idea," he writes. "In light of the fact we are at an impasse of sorts and both James' [Gilliar's] lawyers and my Chairman [Joe] gave an emphatic NO."

(Gilliar's lawyer only said, "It is difficult to comment" about the proposed unequal voting rights, an email on the laptop shows.)

Hunter continues: "I think we should all meet in Romania on Tuesday next week. Zang will be there and so will the completed agreement.... We all want you to be part of this partnership.... The fact that you're even putting up with our cautious schizophrenia—one moment we're competing with Goldman Sachs and the next we're spending hours on why I wasn't invited to a dinner party—must be maddening. You clearly see the path to not just riches but real generational wealth. And I assume that's why you've endured this much brain damage to begin with."

Bobulinski replies: "H—with all [due] respect I think you are misrepresenting what James' lawyer said and it is disheartening u would do such a thing, also am not sure which Chairman you are referencing but they clearly don't understand the agreement as it is written. Not sure why you have such concern with things, but I would chalk it up to you haven't sat down and gone through all the scenarios of the board. James is willing to recuse himself from the vote to remove any perception that he could side with me, so as the vote is defined if something was divided where u, Jim and Rob were on one side and I was on the other side, would encourage u to think of a solution on how you would cure that situation."

Bobulinski makes a jocular suggestion for resolving any deadlock.

"We could arm wrestle for it, play bingo, have your Chairman [Joe] weigh in or something else that is fair and neutral to both sides."

Hunter doesn't see the humor: "Well Tony it may just be the time of night or one too many drinks but your trying to be funny is lost on me and probably most people who don't fall at the high end of the Aspergers spectrum. I'll say it one final time. I don't care how much money or how many soulless oligarchs you call friend.

"Money doesn't interest me, winning is ephemeral and fleeting and I have no interest spending my days on a super yacht measuring my dick with the people on the super yacht next to me.

"I care about one thing. My family. And your demands make me uncomfortable and your insults remind me of the shit the captain of the lacrosse team said to me in college about my dad right before I broke his fucking jaw."

Bobulinski, the strongly built former wrestler, replies: "Keep at it H! That is exactly the point. I and all the partners around the table are trying to protect u and your family! Way more than you...understand, but do please come to Monaco, I'll give you 3 cracks at trying to break mv jaw before I respond."

At this point Biden family friend Walker has had enough: "Please stop."

In the next group chat Bobulinski tries to mollify Hunter: "If you are so worried about your family, you wouldn't be doing this because as u said, all of your dad's lawyers and any lawyer would advise you and Jim not to touch this with a 100-foot pole so if you are willing to take risk so be it. I am willing to stand by your side and take risk as well but there has to be balance in governance and the board."

Walker tries to excuse Hunter's churlishness in a message to Bobulinski: "When he said his chairman, he was talking about his dad and I think your dismissal of it maybe offended him a bit, but you didn't know what he was talking about. Let's let it go till the morning if we can."

Bobulinski replies: "Of course but if his dad really read the agreement, he would support it in a second. That's actually my point."

The following week Bobulinski will fly to Romania to meet Director Zang, but Hunter won't join them. Instead, they arrange to catch up afterward in Monte Carlo, where Hunter is due at a Burisma board meeting with Ukrainian oligarch Mykola Zlochevsky.

17

In Bed with Xi and Putin

"Nothing was unethical."
—Joe Biden defending Hunter, October 2020

Hunter flies into Monaco on June 2, 2017, for a board meeting of Burisma, the corrupt Ukrainian energy company that cut his $83,333 monthly director fees in half two months after his father left office.

Hallie was supposed to accompany him, but they have just broken up after he accused her of cheating on him with one of his brother's friends.

"I cannot believe you are saying we are finished. And in a text," Hallie messages him before he gets on the overnight flight from Dulles airport.

"Why you choose David over me, I don't know…and that's what hurts the most," he replies. "The realization that I didn't and still don't deserve the respect you showed my brother."

He is met at the Nice Cote d'Azur Airport at 7:30 a.m. on that sunny Friday by a Burisma limousine and private security detail.

"Welcome to Monaco!" emails Burisma executive Vadym Pozharskyi. "Happy you are arriving. The driver and security will take you to the Hermitage where you can leave your bags and change. He will wait for you and will take you to us at the yacht club."

The Hôtel Hermitage, a Belle Epoque palace overlooking Monaco Harbor and the Mediterranean, is a five-minute walk up the hill from the Monaco Yacht Club, where Burisma is holding its second "Energy Security Forum," a reputation-polishing event attended by as many former heads of state as the dapper Pozharskyi can rustle up.

In a coup for Burisma, the forum will be opened that morning by Prince Albert II, head of the Princely House of Grimaldi and son of the late Prince Rainier III and Grace Kelly.

Hunter's benefactor, Ukrainian oligarch Mykola Zlochevsky, the owner of Burisma, is waiting for him at the yacht club, sporting a silk burgundy jacket stretched across his boxy frame, an open-necked white shirt, a new closely trimmed black beard, a shaved head tanned by the Riviera sun, and an enormous sapphire and diamond ring on his left hand.

He is attentive to Hunter but he speaks little English, only Russian and Ukrainian, and has to wear special translation headphones to listen to the speeches that day.

This year, instead of going to Zlochevsky's cocktail reception after the forum, Hunter arranges to meet Tony Bobulinski, who is in Monte Carlo for the Grand Prix.

Hunter tells his partner to rendezvous on the patio outside the Hermitage. He says he is going to climb out the window of his hotel room, to evade Burisma's security detail. (Why he feels he has to sneak past his Ukrainian bodyguards he doesn't explain. But he once complained to a friend about his father controlling him through his Secret Service detail, "guys that he got their daughter into the naval academy that he had to the VP residence and let them use his apartment to stay and cost the White House, guys he paid their health insurance premiums for anonymously. All those guys they were made aware I was around and they were supposed to look out [for] me.")

Bobulinski goes to the patio at the allotted time, but Hunter never arrives and doesn't answer his phone. After waiting more than an hour, Bobulinski leaves in disgust, assuming he has fallen asleep.

Photographs on Hunter's laptop late that night appear to be taken aboard Zlochevsky's yacht looking out on Monaco Harbor.

Privately, Bobulinski expresses frustration to Gilliar about Hunter. "He is a complete fuck up. Really have zero interest in being partners with him. His family is getting crazier and crazier."

Three months later, the skipped meeting still a sore point, Bobulinski makes a snide remark and Hunter explodes.

"Fuck you tony i wasn't asleep," he writes on WhatsApp. "I was on nikolay's [an alternative spelling sometimes used for Zlochevsky's first name] boat arguing about my position in the kazak deal and it was heated—jesus you play this bs card all the time—and exactly what other meeting have i ever missed Tony?

"…I sincerely do not like you as a human being. You're a bully with an inferiority complex…. I couldn't call because I was fighting for the only income I have left right now from Burisma. It was a very heated and very tense and extremely unavoidable negotiation."

After Monte Carlo, Hunter and Hallie reconcile and rent a $5 million waterfront house in Annapolis, Maryland. Nestled among crepe myrtles and hydrangeas on the banks of the Severn River, it has a pool for Hallie's kids and a private jetty to moor Hunter's twenty-seven-foot Grady-White.

Hunter is still complaining about Ye's no-show in New York, so Gilliar drafts a letter for him to send to the Chairman.

"It was my great disappointment to have missed you on your last visit to the United States but please accept my best wishes from my family and I, and our partners at SinoHawk," says the letter written in Hunter's name. "We are all hoping to see you here again soon in NYC or in Shanghai."

The point of the letter is to get CEFC to pay up for the past two years of work done by the Biden family and their associates. Now that Joe has left office, payment is due: "I hope you are very happy with the progress that has been made in Oman.... We would like to bring those deals to closure and as per our discussions."

It concludes on the "top relationship" Hunter has "with the leaders both politically and economically in countries you are interested in expanding into in the coming months and years."

At about the same time, he and Uncle Jim are cooking up a sneaky side deal with CEFC, which Hunter describes as "a $4 billion deal to build the fucking largest fucking LNG port in the world" on Monkey Island in Louisiana to ship liquefied natural gas to China. Jim tells Hunter this is the deal that will finally make them rich.

Chairman Ye and Director Zang have bigger fish to fry, however.

They are working on China's biggest investment in Russia to date, a $9 billion acquisition of the Russian state oil giant Rosneft that signals a tectonic shift in geopolitical power.

Relations between Moscow and the West had soured after Russia's annexation of Crimea in March 2014, invasion of Ukraine and the downing of Malaysian flight MH17 over eastern Ukraine by what Dutch investigators concluded was a surface-to-air missile supplied to pro-Russian rebels.

The subsequent US and European Union sanctions against Russia saw a cash-strapped Putin move closer to Xi, and in May 2014, the two leaders struck a $400 billion deal for Russia to deliver natural gas to China.

Now, in 2017, China wants to buy a stake in Russia's national oil and gas company, and CEFC is right in the middle of it.

This is not just a Belt and Road acquisition of a traditional oil company, but the marriage of an arm of the Russian state with the CCP.

A personal triumph for Xi, the deal will cement the Sino-Russia alliance and be a poke in the eye of America's national interest. The Trump administration will use every tool at its disposal to undermine it.

It's a high stakes play for Hunter's partner.

Gilliar tells Bobulinski that Chairman Ye will meet with Vladimir Putin to progress the deal, but he is waiting for the green light from President Xi—whom he calls "No. 1."

"As far as I know chairman [Ye] will come to meet VP [Putin] if he gets approval from no. 1 [Xi]," writes Gilliar in a WhatsApp message on May 17, 2017. "Otherwise, he wouldn't. He's not traveling much. I will check all by time u are up."

Chairman Ye does fly to Moscow on June 14, to meet oligarch Igor Sechin; the Rosneft CEO, a Darth Vader to Putin's emperor, had been personally targeted by the US-led sanctions.

On July 4, President Xi meets Putin in Moscow, where they announce a $10 billion investment fund for Belt and Road infrastructure projects. Putin seals the deal by bestowing on Xi the Russian government's most prestigious honor, the Order of St. Andrew the Apostle.

Zang also is in Moscow, from July 4 until July 7. Within weeks, Reuters will report that CEFC is set to acquire a 14 percent stake in Rosneft.

On August 28, Zang appears in a photograph with Putin at the World Judo Championships in Budapest. The two men stand side by side wearing red ties and slight smiles, Zang looming large over the diminutive Russian.

It is an indication of the importance of CEFC, since Putin is not in the habit of random photo opportunities with Chinese businessmen. The photograph soon vanishes from the Chinese website where it appeared on August 29.

But screenshots are preserved by associates of Hunter as evidence of the shocking fact that President Biden, his son Hunter, and his brother Jim had a partner doing business, not just with China's Xi Jinping, but with Russia's Vladimir Putin.

18

All the Trouble in the World

*"The Bidens are the best I know at doing exactly what
the Chairman wants from this partnership."*
—Hunter to Chinese partner Gongwen Dong, August 2017

The day that CEFC officially announces the $9 billion Rosneft deal, September 8, 2017, Hunter goes on a spending spree.

A $100,000 line of credit for Hunter, his uncle Jim and aunt Sara, under the name Hudson West III, has been set up by CEFC's Gonweng Dong, who approves the Biden trio as "authorized users of credit cards associated with the account."

They immediately start buying airline tickets, technology products, and hotel rooms, all transactions flagged for "potential financial criminal activity," the Senate inquiry will report.

Hunter emails a real estate agent to ask about buying a $4 million waterfront house in Annapolis, not far from where he and Hallie are renting.

Later that month he is in New York, shopping. He outlays $14,115 on his platinum Amex at luxury menswear store Riflessi on "Billionaire's Row," 57th Street. He spends $7,694.90 at Caruso Men's Wear and $537.34 at Brooks Brothers.

He has to look the part for a black-tie dinner for the National Committee on American Foreign Policy on September 26, at the Metropolitan Club. Founded in 1891 by Gilded Age financier John Pierpont Morgan for wealthy friends such as the Vanderbilts and the Whitneys, and housed in the city's grandest marble palazzo on the corner of Fifth Avenue and East 60th Street.

From the sublime to Hell's Kitchen, Hunter also drops $12,000 dollars that month at Larry Flint's Hustler Club on 12th Avenue, just a mile from the Mandarin Oriental Hotel where he and Uncle Jim are guaranteed the corporate rate of $2,995 per night for a Central Park View Suite.

Ye's emissaries, Dong and Yan, have set him up with a New York office at 40 West 57th Street, above Robert De Niro's Japanese fusion restaurant Nobu Fifty Seven, where a plump appetizer-sized wedge of miso-glazed black cod will set you back $43.

Close by are the offices of Smile Design Manhattan, where Hunter will spend $69,977 over the next two months getting his teeth fixed, after years of drug abuse have caused them to rot.

But storm clouds are gathering on the horizon, as the new Trump administration adopts an aggressive approach to national security threats from China.

Suddenly, Director Zang is having visa trouble.

On September 11, 2017, Uncle Jim emails Hunter urgently: "Director Visa. Call."

Two weeks later, Bobulinski tells Biden partner Rob Walker: "Director Zang his wife and kids visas were all denied. Neither of them can get in touch with Hunter and Jim. Zang's kid was supposed to come here to school but didn't show."

Bobulinski raises the issue with Hunter the following month: "Director had his visa denied 3x and his kids and wife's visas denied 3x."

"I know," replies Hunter. "We are out of it per the instructions of the Chairman last time I saw him."

The Spence School on the Upper East Side, where Rouqi Zang was enrolled, emails Uncle Jim to ask what has happened to the Zangs.

"They paid their tuition for the year," writes Susan Parker, director of admissions. "They kept in touch for a while telling us about Rouqi's visa problems etc. In the past few weeks, though, they have stopped responding to our emails—we have lost contact."

Over that summer, Ye has been inviting Hunter to his new penthouse on Central Park West and expressing concern that federal law enforcement agencies are investigating him, Hunter will tell the *New Yorker*. Ye offers him $1 million to be his "private counsel."

The "Attorney Engagement Letter," which Ye's lieutenant Dong emails Hunter on September 10. describes the role as "Counsel to matters related to US law and advice pertaining to the hiring and legal analysis of any US Law Firm or Lawyer."

Hunter will receive the $1 million six months later, in a wire sent from Hudson West III to Owasco, but it is not Chairman Ye's name on the label. The wire is for "Dr Patrick Ho Chi Ping Representation."

Patrick Ho, sixty-nine, is the former Hong Kong politician who ran Ye's promotional arm, the nonprofit China Energy Fund Committee (CEFC), which enjoyed the privilege of "special consultative status" at the United Nations.

On November 18, 2017, just two months after the Rosneft deal was announced, Ho is arrested at JFK airport by federal agents from the Southern District of New York and is charged with attempting to bribe African government officials.

The bribery was business as usual for CEFC, but this time Ho had come up against an incorruptible leader. In December 2014, Ho flew to Chad with $2 million in cash stashed in eight gift boxes, which he tried to give to President Idriss Déby. The bribe was for CEFC to secure oil rights in the impoverished central African nation.

Déby rejected the money. The move ultimately would lead to Ye's downfall, and the collapse of Hunter and Uncle Jim's most promising get-rich-quick scheme, although the Bidens did manage to extract more than $6 million from CEFC before the end.

After his arrest, the first call Ho makes from the Metropolitan Correctional Center in lower Manhattan is to Jim Biden.

Uncle Jim will tell the *New York Times* the next year that he was surprised at Ho's call and thought it must have been meant for Hunter. So he passed on his nephew's contact information.

"There is nothing else I have to say," Jim is quoted saying. "I don't want to be dragged into this any more."

What the Times doesn't know is that Jim has admitted to Biden lawyer George Mesires that he has met Ho.

After Ho's arrest, Hunter's CEFC-appointed executive assistant, JiaQi Bao, twenty-nine, emails him to express shock at the Southern District's global reach.

"On Dr Ho...I just don't get it, why the US has the legitimacy or the authority to sue when whatever involved is not happening in the US and no US company is involved? If someone really should sue, it should be Hong Kong or the African country...how is this has anything to do with the US?"

The answer is that the new Trump administration has marked President Xi's Belt and Road activities as economic aggression that threatens America's national security.

Trump's first attorney general, Jeff Sessions, has directed the Department of Justice to prioritize the investigation and prosecution of Chinese companies for trade secret theft, economic espionage, and offenses under the Foreign Corrupt Practices Act. It will also enforce the Foreign Agents Registration Act, a law enacted in 1938 against Nazi influence.

Another blow follows for CEFC. Six days after Ho's arrest, Ye's $100 million deal to buy a stake in New York brokerage firm Cowen Inc. collapses, after failing to win approval from the newly vigilant CFIUS.

It's all bad news for Chairman Ye—and for the Biden family business.

Unusually for a bribery case, Ho will be denied bail. Despite the $1 million retainer, Hunter does not appear to perform any legal work.

But on the afternoon of Ho's arrest, he engages the attorney who will represent Ho, Edward Kim, of Fifth Avenue firm Krieger Kim & Lewin.

He also contacted the FBI on Ho's behalf, according to an email from Edward Kim that day: "If you're able to find the names of the FBI agents you spoke with that would be helpful."

Three days later, Kim emails CEFC's Dong cost estimates for legal fees based on white-collar trials prosecuted in the Southern District, the legendary US Attorney's Office on which the TV series "Billions" is based. Kim cites as an example *US v. Raj Rajaratnam*, the largest hedge fund insider trading scheme in US history. Hedge fund manager Rajaratnam forked out $70 million in legal fees but still spent eleven years in prison.

As the noose begins to tighten around Chairman Ye in the late summer of 2017, Hunter's crack addiction is spiraling out of control.

He spends $14,100 at the luxury Passages Malibu Addiction Treatment Center just before Ho is arrested in November but relapses within weeks.

The home front is stormy, too: "I'm blowing the whole thing up," he texts Hallie on November 3.

Hallie: "Stop! Leave me alone!"

Hunter: "I'm leaving. I'm sorry I've ruined your life Hallie, but you win whatever game you were playing when you told me you loved me. You have finally fucking broken me."

Hallie: "You are not listening to EVERYONE around you. The world is not against you, not lying to you, not betraying you…. Your anger and blame are what is killing us. Stop acting like a child. I love you but I can't take what you are doing to me."

Hunter also is fighting with his long-time factotum Eric Schwerin.

In December 2017, as Schwerin is trying to extricate himself from Rosemont Seneca, Hunter emails: "We are no longer just done as business partners you should consider moving to somewhere in Florida I'll never go. Naples is perfect—you can live in perpetual timeshare with your parents and talk about what a horrible person I am."

Whatever troubles Hunter has, they are nothing compared to Chairman Ye's.

In late February, three months after Ho's conviction, Ye reportedly was detained in Shanghai, on suspicion of "economic crimes," and disappeared.

Within months of his disappearance, President Xi's beloved Rosneft deal has collapsed, and the Chinese will have to pay the Russians $250 million compensation.

Ye may have had an inkling that the Sino-Russian venture was jinxed back in October 2017, when he wrote an uncharacteristically reflective statement on the company's WeChat account, to mark CEFC's sealing of the Rosneft deal.

He begins by expressing "pride" in the deal and pledges his continued "determination to implement the Belt and Road Initiative at all costs."

But then he sounds an ominous note: "I'm not here to celebrate my achievements today, but to warn of failure. When you become the focus, it means that every word and deed will be amplified, especially [if] you have unconsciously offended people. When you climb to the top of the mountain…it means that you have no way to go up. There may be cliffs on all three sides, and a mistake will become eternal hatred. If the top of the mountain is in the severe winter, once you are slow, you will soon freeze and become a specimen of failure."

He won't be heard from again.

His wife, children, and mother are safe in New York. But Ye has met the fate of many a highflyer who falls out of favor with President Xi.

———•◦•———

A few weeks after Ye's disappearance, his lieutenant Mervyn Yan emails Hunter to say that new Chinese administrators have taken over CEFC: "The headquarters called a meeting today to ask for updates of JVs. In short, all others have been closed and money returned to headquarters except this one.

"If you want to keep this one we must demonstrate it's operating. We need to have weekly or biweekly summaries of business meetings, projects discussed etc. Otherwise, they have legitimate reason to shut down this company."

Hunter's adoring CEFC-appointed assistant JiaQi Bao writes him a long email on March 31 to encourage him to extract maximum advantage from the situation.

"I'm a bit hesitated to say this to you, because I don't want you to misunderstood me as a messed up bad girl. However...here is my two cents: Whatever money from Hudson West, please take [as] much as possible.... It doesn't matter whether [it] is labeled as 'personal goodwill/ loan' or 'non-recourse,' ...."

"Whatever agreement or labels of the money doesn't mean anything, especially because Ye's situation changed.... So take whatever money you can take...before any restriction levied by Chinese regulators."

She also asks how she should return "your doggy chain necklace.... Don't be a stranger. I still owe you a home-cooked Chinese dinner."

She doesn't need to tell Hunter to take the money and run. He and Uncle Jim are in a mad scramble to salvage whatever they can before CEFC sinks.

But Yan has started querying Hunter's expenses.

"At a first glance, [a lot is] not business related. Kevin will not sign off on these," Yan writes in an email on March 14, 2018. "Can we have our back-office accountants sort out these tomorrow? We need the invoice receipts."

Hunter doesn't take it well: "As for a CEFC accountant going over my expense report I will personally sue you Kevin and the accountant if you forward my expense report to them....

"I am the managing director of CEFC. I have complete authority as to who I hire and who I fire....

"If you refuse to sign the wire Kevin I will seek to have you removed from the board.... I will bring suit in the Chancery Court in Delaware [where] I am privileged to have worked with and know every judge on the chancery court....

"If my expenses as submitted are not wired into the Owasco account today I will file an injunction to freeze all Hudson West accounts."

Dong replies coolly: "You have been reimbursed more than $220,000 for July to September expenses…. No matter what [was] the agreement between you and your friend [Chairman Ye]…I must be responsible to execute the agreement in a professional way….

"Please rectify the expense report. I hope you can understand…. You cannot sue us for not paying incorrect expenses."

It's as close to rude as Dong ever gets. But it's a far cry from the deference shown to Hunter by the Chinese when his father was vice president and he was flying high on his personal relationship with Chairman Ye.

Unbeknownst to Bobulinski, Hunter went behind his back a few months after they signed the SinoHawk joint venture with Director Zang in New York in May 2017.

He and Uncle Jim Biden set up a separate joint venture with CEFC in August to do a deal he told the Chinese was "so much more interesting to me and my family" than SinoHawk.

On August 2, he emails Ye's lieutenants, Dong and Yan, telling them that the Chairman's original offer in Miami was to pay his family $30 million "for introductions alone" but that the offer since had been upgraded to an even sweeter payoff.

"My Understanding is that the original agreement with the Director was for consulting fees based on introductions alone—a rate of $10M per year for a three-year guarantee total of $30M," writes Hunter.

"The chairman changed that deal after we met in Miami TO A MUCH MORE LASTING AND LUCRATIVE ARRANGEMENT to create a holding company 50% percent owned by ME and 50% owned by him….

"The reason this proposal by the chairman was so much more interesting to me and my family is that we would also be partners in the equity and profits of the JV's [joint venture's] investments."

Dong appears confused about the new arrangement, so the following day Hunter writes him an irritated email: "I am tired of this Kevin. I can make $5M in salary at any law firm in America.

"If you think this is about money, it's not. The Bidens are the best I know at doing exactly what the Chairman wants from this partnership. Please let's not quibble over peanuts."

The money starts hitting Hunter's bank account two days later. SinoHawk will never see a penny.

CEFC Infrastructure Investment, a subsidiary of CEFC, sends $100,000 to Hunter's law firm Owasco, on August 4, 2017, according to records obtained by the Grassley-Johnson Senate inquiry.

"This transaction was identified for potential criminal financial activity," the inquiry found, drawing on confidential "suspicious activity reports" that banks are required to file with the Treasury Department when they spot an irregular transaction.

On August 8, CEFC wires $5 million to Hudson West III, a company incorporated in Delaware by the Chinese the previous April, which Hunter and Uncle Jim are using for their CEFC side hustle.

This is the $5 million Bobulinski has been waiting for, the loan signed off on in May by Hunter and Director Zang that would pay for Oneida's 50 percent capital contribution to the SinoHawk joint venture.

Every month for more than a year, Hudson West III sends payments labelled "consulting fees" to Hunter's firm Owasco until the total amounts to $4,790,375.25. Hudson West III also sends more than $76,000 to Uncle Jim's firm, Lion Hall Group, with the label: "office expense and reimbursement."

All this money has raised a flag with Hunter's bank. On September 13, 2018, Edward Prewitt, Hunter's long-suffering wealth adviser, emails him questions from the Wells Fargo corporate compliance team about "the purpose of incoming wires from Hudson West" to Owasco.

Hunter answers that he is "Chairman and partner" of Hudson West III. The incoming wires are my monthly and the monthly fee of James Biden who is a...consultant to the company."

The bank also notes that Hunter's Owasco accounts "appear to fund primarily personal expenses." It queries the bona fides of Uncle Jim and Aunt Sara's firm, the Lion Hall Group, noting the owner is a "relative

[and] the address appears to be a residential address. What is the business type?"

Hunter replies: "Lion Hall is operated out of the separate office structure on that property and has a sole employee...James Biden my uncle with whom I have been doing business with for well over a decade."

Over the next year, Hunter will move $1.4 million from Owasco to his uncle's account, sending twenty wires between August 14, 2017, and August 3, 2018.

These transactions "were identified for potential criminal financial activity," the Senate inquiry will report: "When the bank contacted Sara Biden regarding the overall wire activity, she stated...the Lion Hall Group was assisting Owasco with an international client through a contract that had since terminated.... Sara Biden told the bank that she would not provide any supporting documentation, and she also refused to provide additional information to more clearly explain the activity. Consequently, the bank submitted the account for closure."

Bobulinski had suspected for over a year that Hunter and Jim had done a back door deal with the Chinese.

None of the money promised by CEFC for SinoHawk had materialized, and he got the runaround from the Chinese whenever he asked about it.

Director Zang blamed the delay wiring the money on "the risk management department of CEFC," Bobulinski told Gilliar in a WhatsApp message on July 26, 2017.

"Chairman Ye and Director Zang [say they still] fully support the framework of establishing the joint venture, based on their trust on BD [Biden] family."

But Bobulinski was starting to puzzle over the financing: "$5 million is lent to BD [Biden] family.... How will this $5 million be used (or the 10 million as a whole)? This 5 million loan to BD family is interest-free. But if the 5M is used up, should CEFC keep lending more to the family?"

Hunter had been incommunicado for months, but in October 2017, soon after CEFC announced the Rosneft deal, Bobulinski received a WhatsApp message from him, out of the blue.

"What's the word on all the deals you were negotiating? Wow they are taking a long time. Oman? Luxembourg? Russia? I've simply stayed out of the Russia mess. And I just assumed you're plugging away."

Bobulinski replies: "When was the last time u saw the chairman? Zang created a mess w that Rosneft deal. Pics of him w Putin all over the place."

Hunter: "Well that's actually good for us. Chinese bailing out feckless Putin, [Zang] sticking it to him through the pictures along with Xi. They're saying [to Russia] you're just another business partner now—here hang this on your office wall."

Bobulinski: "So you 1000% didn't reach out to Chairman Ye or Director Zang and create parallel noise?"

Hunter: "No. I've been talking to the Chairman on a regular basis. I was his first guest at his new apartment. He cooked me lunch himself and we ate in the kitchen together. He has me helping him on a number of his personal [issues] (staff visas and some more sensitive things).... He and I discussed the Rosneft deal and he is pissed off but only by the exception which I guess was Zang's deal. Anyway, he and I are solid.... We have a standing once a week call as I am also his personal counsel (we signed an attorney client engagement letter) in the US."

Bobulinski: "Well he has not funded the $10MM.... When did you sign a US attorney client engagement letter?"

Hunter: "US attorney??? What do you mean? I'm his lawyer in the US. Never talked to him about your deals. I said 'I haven't' engaged with Zang in months. I only talk to the Chairman and in person. I assumed you lost interest as we haven't spoken for so long."

Bobulinski: "About 'my deals' they apparently are our deals, not my deals. HB—not much for games.... They were supposed to fund $10MM USD into Sinohawk accounts. You know that!... The Wall Street Journal has been fighting to get a hold of the Sinohawk documents to tie u to the Chairman given the Rosneft deal and your father."

On December 4, 2018, CEFC pays Bobulinski $50,000 compensation.

When the Grassley-Johnson report, "Hunter Biden, Burisma, and Corruption," is published in September 2020, Bobulinski's suspicions are confirmed. The report reveals the existence of two wires from CEFC sending $6 million to Biden family loyalist Rob Walker.

Bobulinski instantly realizes that this was the money that was supposed to have been paid by CEFC to SinoHawk.

Furious at the alleged deception, he gives Jim Biden a piece of his mind.

"The fact that you and HB [Hunter] were lying to Rob, James and I while accepting $5 million from CEFC is infuriating," he messages Uncle Jim. "Oh, and congrats on Joe's nomination."

19

The Spy Chief of China

"The richest man in the world is missing, who was my partner."
—**Hunter to a friend, voice memo May 11, 2018**

N*ew York Times* reporter David Barboza emails Hunter's lawyer George Mesires on December 4, 2018, for comment on a story relating to Patrick Ho's bribery trial, which was underway in New York.

Four reporters have been working for months on an investigation into Ho's controller, Chairman Ye, and his cultivation of Washington powerbrokers such as Joe and Hunter Biden.

This rare media interest in their business affairs has been a source of intense angst for the Bidens since they were first tipped off in July. All summer, Hunter had accused people of leaking to the *Times*, including the loyal Rob Walker. "The information this reporter has comes directly from James [Gilliar] or you," Hunter texts. "I hope to god it's not you—that would fully and completely break my heart."

When Mesires texts him about the *Times'* inquiries on December 4, Hunter is in Newburyport, Massachusetts, undergoing an unusual addiction treatment program in which he receives daily intravenous infusions of the horse tranquilizer ketamine, while at night he smokes crack and entertains prostitutes.

Mesires wants to update him on his efforts to hose down the *Times'* story: "Barboza said that there is 'very little about Hunter, because as it turns out, CEFC tried to talk to a lot of people in Washington.'"

The other good news: "No reference to Joe Biden specifically relative to CEFC's efforts."

Barboza has told Mesires the story will contain, "Three references to Biden: the first reference is at the beginning of the story that asserts that CEFC/Ye was…'at some point negotiating a business deal with the family of the Vice President….'

"Second reference is [about] Patrick Ho's arrest. Apparently, the reporters learned from covering the court case…Ho's 'first call' following his arrest was to one of the Bidens. Specifically, to Jim Biden. The story will quote Jim who said that…Ho's call was probably intended for Hunter, not Jim, although Jim Biden admits that he believes that he has met Mr Ho….

"Third reference: 'In 2016, a Ye aide met with Hunter Biden in Washington, and then in May 2017, the Chairman himself met with Hunter privately in a hotel in Miami where he proposed a deal to invest in US energy and infrastructure projects…. As far as we know, no business transaction ever took place nor was an arrangement ever made.'"

When the *Times* story is published on December 12, 2018, the Biden family is prominent in the headline: "Chinese Tycoon Sought Power and Influence…Ye Jianming courted the Biden family and networked with former US security officials. Today, his empire is crashing down in court."

Hunter is in New York to meet his father and Doug Brinkley, the CNN historian, "who is a friend and tried to get me to run the JFK library," he tells his therapist.

Hunter texts Mesires about the *Times'* story: "Why put me in the lead. Assholes."

"It makes it sexy," Mesires replies. "I think it's all pretty diluted considering all the other names that CEFC reached out to."

Hunter: "I just hate being used up front for no good reason.... It makes me once again look like I'm taking advantage and have no ethics and I'm at best a dupe and worse a dishonor to my name. I'm being dramatic.... In fact you did an incredible job of keeping this basically to a big fat nothing."

Mesires: "At the end of the day, I think people jadedly say 'this is how the world works.'

"You are an asset to your family's name and if anything you need a PR agent. Get back on the board of a non-profit. Show everyone how fucking smart and insightful you are and don't look back at any historic headline. They're whores. I'm surprised they didn't run a picture of you because it would sell more papers you handsome bastard."

The next day, in the Daniel Patrick Moynihan Courthouse in lower Manhattan, Ho is convicted of bribery and money laundering, without calling a single witness.

Federal investigators had prosecuted him with "particular zeal," the *Wall Street Journal* reported, and placed the spotlight on China's use of foreign bribery to win contracts for President Xi's Belt and Road Initiative.

Ho complains in an email to a friend during the trial that he is the "first of the sacrificial lambs" of America's new "hostility" to China.

"The storm is just starting to whip up to a roaring disaster. Brace yourself for the darkest moment before dawn."

Ho's defense during the jury trial had been to paint payments to officials in Chad and Uganda as charitable corporate donations by a man on a patriotic mission to generate goodwill about Belt and Road.

"Dr Ho and his colleagues asked for nothing in return," his lawyer told the jury. "His job was to network and build good will."

Prosecutors accused Ho of seeking to secure unfair business advantages for CEFC and said he was operating at the direction of Chairman

Ye, who sought to corrupt foreign officials with cash and a promise that they—and their families—would share in CEFC's future profits.

"Corruption is an insidious plague…found in all countries, big and small, rich and poor," Judge Loretta Preska said when she sentenced Ho to three years in prison, after which he would be deported to Hong Kong. "But it is in the developing world that its effects are most destructive."

Hunter has spent most of the year on an extended drug bender in Los Angeles, where he fled in April, after Chairman Ye disappeared in Shanghai and CEFC collapsed.

He will reflect on the frightening turn his life has taken in a voice memo titled "Most Genius Shit Ever Made" on his laptop, recorded in Los Angeles on May 11, 2018.

"I get calls from my father to tell me the *New York Times* is calling," he tells a stripper friend. Neil Young's "Harvest Moon" plays in the background amid the sounds of smoking and kissing.

"I have another *New York Times* reporter calling about my representation of Patrick Ho, literally the fucking spy chief of China who started the company that my partner [Chairman Ye], who is worth $323 billion, founded and is now missing. The richest man in the world is missing, who was my partner.

"He was missing since I last saw him in his $58 million apartment inside a $4 billion deal to build the fucking largest fucking LNG port in the world and I am receiving calls from the Southern District of New York, from the US attorney himself. My best friend in business Devon has named me as a witness, without telling me, in a criminal case…. I'm talking about a fucking criminal case in which Devon has named me as a witness."

Hunter's life is a mess, but it will only get worse that year in L.A., as his crack addiction spirals out of control, he has close shaves with the law, and he seethes with anger and resentment over real and imagined grievances against family and friends.

He is putting at risk his father's last chance to run for president, but he is at the point where he doesn't care.

Uncle Jim, the only person in his life he never fights with, tries to placate him: "Everyone loves you, but who in this F' up family has treated you with respect," Uncle Jim writes in an email.

"You give and give and, the question on everyone's lips is 'How is Hunter.' What the hell, what do people expect of you? By trying to mend our broken family, you have put yourself in a corner. Enough is enough. Stop beating yourself up. A finer person I have never met."

In September, his half-sister Ashley, thirty-seven, texts him.

"I hesitate to write you this. Because your response is unpredictable. But I can't help but plead to you to get well.

"Our father is devastated. His personality has fundamentally changed without you by his side. He is constantly sad and down. It pains me to see him and our entire family like this...praying, hoping, begging you to come back to us."

Finally, when Hunter goes home to his parents' house for Christmas, his family will stage an intervention.

"I'm in the middle of an intervention, Bri, the whole family," he texts a female friend waiting for him in a hotel.

Brianna: "You got sober?... Do I leave or stay?"

Hunter: "I'm sorry Brianna, my girls, my sister, my parents, my uncle. I'm going to 30-day inpatient."

He describes the raw scene in his memoir. His entire family waiting for him with two drug addiction counselors, when he arrives.

"Not fucking this," he says and bolts.

Joe chases his son down the driveway: "He grabbed me, swung me around, and hugged me. He held me tight in the dark and cried for the longest time."

Hunter agrees to go to a rehab facility in Maryland, but as soon as he is dropped off, he calls an Uber and checks into a hotel near Baltimore airport.

"I sat in my room and smoked the crack I'd tucked away in my traveling bag."

Joe only has four months left to announce his candidacy for the 2020 election. Something has to be done about Hunter.

CHAPTER

Falling Apart

"I'm so sad that I sullied my brother's memory by starting all of this."
—Hunter to Hallie Biden, May 24, 2017

Hunter was living in a beautiful $16,000-a-month four-bedroom oceanfront at Malibu, spending his days smoking crack and entertaining escorts.

But for some reason, on October 12, 2018, he went home to Delaware and bought a gun.

It was a .38-caliber revolver from StarQuest Shooters & Survival Supply in Wilmington, a ten-minute drive from his father's house.

On the Firearms Transaction Record he signed that day Hunter responded "No" to a question that asked, "Are you an unlawful user of, or addicted to, marijuana or any depressant, stimulant, narcotic drug, or any other controlled substance?"

Lying on that federal background check form is a felony, for which other people have been jailed.

Hunter was obviously a major drug user. He admits he was a crack addict in his memoir and a photo of him asleep with a glass "crack pipe" in his mouth was taken in Malibu just eight days beforehand.

The night before he bought the gun, Hunter was at Hallie's place trawling through her at&t cordless phone. He took forty-nine photographs of the Caller ID display showing incoming numbers for the previous seventeen days.

Late that night he was looking up phone numbers on the people search site Spokeo.com and found a forty-seven-year-old man named Adam from a nearby suburb. He added the screenshot to his photo roll.

Less than two weeks later, on October 23, 2018, Hallie took the gun out of Hunter's pickup and threw it in an open trash can outside Janssen's gourmet grocery market in their local Greenville Center strip mall in Wilmington. The mall is across the road from a high school, so the potential dangers were obvious.

Hunter took up the story in emails he sent to Hallie's older sister Liz Secundy, forty-nine: "She stole my gun out of my truck lock box and threw [it] in a garbage can full to the top at Janssens. Then told me it was my problem to deal with. Then when the police, the FBI, the secret service came on the scene she said she took it from me because she was scared I would harm myself due to my drug and alcohol problem and our volatile relationship and that she was afraid for the kids.

"Really not joking, the cop kept me convinced that Hallie was implying she was scared of me."

He repeated the story to his therapist Keith Ablow: "Did I tell you what she did with my .38?… I freaked when I saw it was missing 10 mins after she took it and when she went back to get it after I scared the shit out of her it was gone which led to state police investigating me. True story."

When the Delaware State Police interviewed Hunter outside Janssen's he told them he used the gun for "target practice," according to a police report obtained by Politico in March 2021.

Asked if the gun had been used in a crime, Hunter "became very agitated," the report said.

When he was asked if he had been doing drugs or drinking heavily, he responded, "Listen, it isn't like that. I think [Hallie] believes I was gonna kill myself."

An officer asked if he had called his father about the incident. Hunter replied, "I have never called my dad for anything."

At roughly the same time, two Secret Service agents arrived at StarQuest Shooters, where Hunter had bought the gun.

"The agents showed their badges and identification cards to [Ron] Palmieri, the store's owner, and asked to take possession of the Firearms Transaction Record that Hunter had filled out to buy the gun earlier that month," Politico reported. "Palmieri refused to hand over the transaction record to the Secret Service agents."

Neither Joe nor Hunter was under Secret Service protection at the time, and the agency denied any involvement.

The missing gun was logged as stolen on the National Crime Information Center website and reportedly was returned later by a man who found it while rummaging in the trash can for recyclables.

No charges were filed against Hunter or Hallie and the incident was not reported in the media until Politico broke the story three years later. But the bizarre episode offered a glimpse into the disintegration of their relationship.

Hunter and his sister-in law began an affair after Beau's death on May 30, 2015. Hunter would confide to friends that she "seduced me…. I started to think of Hallie as the only person in my life who understood my loss."

Hunter's insecurity about his brother emerged in texts to Liz about Hallie's attitude toward him when Beau was dying.

"Hallie told me privately that she turned to me in the hospital during a critical need for a decision and to no one else because she knew Beau wanted me making those decisions for him.

"When I told that to a group of people at a small party explaining how I fell so madly in love with her [for] acknowledging the bond Beau and I had, she laughed and said 'no I did not think that—he would have wanted your dad, of course, but [Joe] was so out of his mind, and I was sobbing and confused, you were the only other person in the room.' Her exact words."

Hunter's sister, Ashley, disapproved of the relationship from the start. On November 11, 2016, two days after Donald Trump's election victory, Ashley sent Hallie a group text, including Joe and Jill.

"You will pay for sitting around while watching my other brother kill himself.… Everyone is talking + Hunter making scenes at restaurants. People are worried. YOU are the problem.… This isn't love. This is my brother high."

Ashley soon sent another group text to Hallie: "Have you lost your damn mind…this isn't how my family operates. You better come to your senses."

Joe weighed in: "Let it go."

Kathleen filed for divorce the following month, and Hunter was bickering with Hallie about whether they should keep their relationship hidden.

"You're right, I just need to calm down, not be so sensitive when you say…that you're embarrassed if I am affectionate with you in public, that you're happy to know people don't know anything about us," he texted Hallie on December 28, 2016.

Two days later, he texted again: "You don't respect me, you're not proud of me and I can understand that. I don't deserve much respect."

By March 2017, Hunter was accusing Hallie of having an affair with a mutual friend, David. She accused him of living a secret life.

"I know you love me and you know I love you desperately," she texted him. "I think you want me AND your dark world where you finally feel free. I don't want to stop you from doing anything that you want to do. You will just resent me, lie and keep it as your secret world. That is not healthy for you or me.… You have filled me completely, but you have other desires. That is ok. It's not bad or wrong, but it just makes me feel bad about myself when I try to accept it."

Hunter's relationship with Hallie's sister Liz, who was separated from her husband, would take a sexual turn. He paid her rent and bought her "panties": "We should shower together by FT [FaceTime] every morning or night when we're up at 3—stress relief—I'll teach you how to masturbate," he texted her.

By May 2017, he was wildly jealous and spying on Hallie's phone: "My God you know how much it hurts to see you called him and texted him…

"I'm so sad that I sullied my brother's memory by starting all of this."

They tried to make a fresh start in a waterfront rental in Annapolis, Maryland. But drug addiction followed them.

A glimpse into their dysfunctional lifestyle came from Ashley, who texted Liz after visiting their house on February 24, 2018.

"This is all getting out of control…. Just came from meeting with police chiefs, and dealers are known in community. Not a good look for the widow of attorney general. Enough is enough…. I was down at the beach and I can promise no one was getting healthy. They left all their drug crap out….

"She is the attorney general's widow, and he is the Vice President's son. If you think that people don't already know everywhere that they are addicted to crack etc. you are naive. When you deal with drug dealers the likelihood of plates being run [police checking car license plates] is high. My dad may run for President and if you think this shit is going to fly?!?! Shit will hit the fan…. The whole town know as do many others. They aren't very discreet. And people are mean….

"And let me tell you they are beyond messy! They left all their drug paraphernalia for my parents to see. It's that bad."

In October 2017, Hunter paid $14,500 for Hallie to go to rehab at Passages, Malibu. But their battles continued.

"Is it helpful that you say I need to make money and feel successful so I can be confident?" Hunter texted Hallie. "$1.6M wasn't good enough for Kathleen and I guess $3M in 9 months isn't good enough for you. You say my penis is average…. You constantly demean me to my family, your family, your friends."

Hallie: "I love you…. I'm not making you feel inadequate or unsuccessful or small or demonized or alone…. I'm not going to argue about something that is not there. Please gain some clarity."

After his Chinese partners met sticky ends, Hunter ran away to Los Angeles in April 2018. But the arguments with Hallie kept raging.

"You are sick, Hunter," Hallie wrote on July 16, 2018. "Abusive and sad. I miss you, not this evil person you are now but the real you who would never treat me or anyone this way. You have mentally and physically abused me Hunter…. I won't tell anyone, but you know the truth. Unless you are completely lying to yourself about who you have become."

———•◦•———

In August 2018, a woman Hunter had met the previous year at the Washington, DC, strip club Mpire—where she worked under the stage name "Dallas"—gave birth to his baby in Arkansas.

Lunden Alexis Roberts, twenty-eight, launched a paternity case the following year. After a DNA sample proved he was the father of the girl, known to the court as NJR, Hunter was ordered to pay child support. But he never acknowledged his child.

"Hunter Biden is…the father of three daughters [and a] son," he will write on the jacket flap of his 2021 memoir, erasing the fourth of his five children.

He claimed of Roberts: "I had no recollection of our encounter."

But the laptop tells a different story.

Hunter knew Roberts well enough to have added her to his phone contacts on June 4, 2017. Three months later, he was sneaking her into his DC office through a back door late at night so often that the House of Sweden's building manager wrote to request he start checking in his after-hours visitors through front-door security.

Hunter fired back a 1,700-word name-dropping diatribe to building manager Cecilia Browning.

He described Roberts in that September 21, 2017, email as "my youngest daughter's basketball mentor. She worked out with Maisy and Sasha Obama when they played in rec league together."

Hunter even appended a "partial bio" of the stripper that included her basketball statistics since high school.

"Lunden is in her final semester at George Washington University's National CSIS Masters Program and ranked #1 in her class," he wrote.

So, his relationship with Roberts was not a fleeting encounter. He was having clandestine assignations with her during a period of at least five months before she became pregnant with his child.

When she was seven months pregnant, she texted that her "due date was Sep 8 2018. All good."

The next month, she texted him the same message four times in a row: "Reached out a few times—it's clear you don't want to be reached. Need to talk to you."

In October, he tried to reconcile with Hallie one last time. But after the gun incident she threw him out.

"I'm done being your excuse to avoid real life, responsibilities reality and sobriety," she texted him on November 4. "Don't come in and out every day and pout that you are not included or respected. You won't be respected by anyone like this."

After escaping his parents' attempt at an intervention that Christmas, he fled to New York, where he ended up at the Yale Club in January 2019.

A former worker at the club says Hunter was notorious for "doing a lot of things that's not supposed to be done but he's a VIP so they didn't do anything.... They cover so much for him."

Hunter's drug dealers would regularly show up, she claimed. "At two in the morning at the service entrance of the club he would get his drug deliveries there. He was too high, and he would come down in his underwear.... He's very classy," she added sarcastically.

But on January 2, Hunter could not persuade his dealer Frankie to deliver his drugs. Frankie told him to meet him downtown at Marquee nightclub.

"I'm outside Marquee," Hunter texts him at 12:38 a.m.

Frankie: "Ask for Jimmy."

Hunter: "I did. They said fuck you. And he just literally threw me out. Fucking took me by the neck and threw me to the ground. I'm going to fucking kill this guy. I mean it Frankie I will have him killed."

Frankie: "Coming out."

Hunter: "If you let me be embarrassed like this I will never fucking talk to you again."

A few minutes later, Hunter texts: "I'm still here Frankie and if you got nothing to say then just get me his name please."

That afternoon, Hunter texts Frankie to say he has a neck injury. "Looks like…I need surgery so thanks a lot Frankie for your concern."

On January 4, Frankie texts to say he will get Hunter the name of the bouncer he claims roughed him up: "He works at Marquee and Avenue. The owners are Noah Tepperberg and Marc Packer."

After a year of debauchery and self indulgence, Hunter is falling apart. Paranoid and angry with the world, his life revolves around crack and Viagra-fueled sex with prostitutes, encounters he often films.

It's worth noting here that, while there is a lot of sexually explicit material on the laptop, nothing indicates that Hunter has an interest in underage girls, despite claims to the contrary.

There is one photo of potential concern in Hunter's image library, of a topless pubescent girl. It is a blurred snap of three teens, taken in the mirror of what looks like a school bathroom. One girl is putting on makeup, another is taking the photo. The third is in the background, reflected in the mirror as she gets dressed, with one breast visible.

The photo was uploaded to the laptop among thousands of images on a shared iCloud account, which included shots of dozens of kids playing sport and clowning around with friends.

Once he discovered the photo, Rudy Giuliani was concerned enough that he brought it to the attention of former NYPD commissioner Bernie Keric, whose advice was that possession of the image could constitute a criminal offense of child pornography under the New York penal code.

This is what prompted Giuliani and Keric to drive to Delaware in October 2020 and hand over a copy of the laptop's hard drive to police.

Concerns also have been raised about messages on the laptop in which Hunter complains that a woman is accusing him of being "sexually inappropriate" with her daughter and of "walking around naked, watching porn, masturbating and doing drugs in front" of the child.

Apart from Hunter's whining, there is no evidence to corroborate the allegation.

"My mom tells [Joe] things like I'm sexually inappropriate with [redacted].... How devastating is that, how completely and utterly demoralized [and] ashamed do you think that makes me feel."

Uncle Jim alludes to the claims in a text. "Your father is getting, as I am, barraged by someone.... We both agree with and trust you.... Once again we both need you [sic] side of the story so we can both shove it down her fucking throat!!!!"

Finally, a photo circulating online is alleged to show an underage female in a sex act with Hunter. But the image is one of a series on the laptop that shows the female, when seen more completely, is an adult.

Child sexual abuse is a horrendous crime that overshadows every other offense, so unfounded allegations not only are unjust but detract from the very real scandals documented on the laptop.

Two weeks after his forty-ninth birthday, Hunter tells his family he is back in rehab, but he is moving around between cheap hotels in New Haven, Connecticut, near Yale, at the time.

Joe has just two months until he has to declare his candidacy for the 2020 election, but his son is a loose cannon.

On February 24, 2019, Hunter is enraged when his father's favorite columnist, Maureen Dowd, writes a piece in the *New York Times*, titled "Uncle Joe's Family Ties." The central topic is "the troubled Hunter."

"Good morning my beautiful son," Joe texts him. "I miss you and love you. Dad."

Hunter lets rip: "Well dad, I guess you were right, if I just didn't... make clear that I never was with Hallie until a year after Beau...it would all just go away like that genius Kate and the rest said it would. Well, having made clear to the world that the only reason for not running is your family problems I'm glad to be the fucking bullseye you painted on my back.

"Oh…good morning…from fucking rehab."

"Kate" is likely to be Kate Bedingfield, Joe Biden's deputy campaign manager.

Hunter keeps raging: "Maureen Dowd points to me as the reason you'll most likely lose it?"

He quotes the column to his father: "It was understandable that, having lost so many close to him, Biden would hold the troubled Hunter tight. And he was doubtless upset about the public nature of the divorce."

Hunter is furious: "The troubled Hunter. This isn't just Kathleen. This is your staff. Don't you not see what just happened? Your team just made me the uncontrollable troubled tax cheat philanderer sex and drug addict that you tried so hard to fix but couldn't. They just totally wrote my life away.

"And if you try and say otherwise, I'll have a hard time understanding how you rationalize this shit…. Well, dad, the truth is, as you and Hallie point out, I am a fucked-up addict that can't be trusted relied upon, nor defended."

About four hours later Hunter writes his dad again: "If you don't run, I'll never have a chance at redemption."

Joe: "I'll run but I need you. H[allie] is wrong."

Next Hunter rages at Hallie: "You seem to have made it out of this relationship clean. The Maureen Dowds of the world and Vanity Fair and all the gossip that you allow about me to be repeated over and over…. I cannot forgive you for saying that you didn't know what other bullshit business deals and other shit that [I was doing]…. I've never done a dishonest business transaction in my life. I'm the most ethical man you will ever know. You say 'shady business deals'?"

Hallie. "Ok then there won't be any articles like that."

H: "Yes that's how it works Hallie. If it's not true they won't write it. You stupid fucking cunt. Everything they've written about me is true. Otherwise, they would never have written it. Hmmmm."

Hallie: "Stop."

Hunter: "So you believe I've had children burned alive in Donetsk."

Hallie: "Your text not making sense."

Hunter: "Or that I had people murdered in Beijing."

Hallie: "I don't know what u are talking about."

Hunter: "They write about it all the time…about how I run a criminal empire."

Hallie: "Just stay sober."

Hunter: "That I'm worth billions of dollars. That I fund the entire democratic elite machine…. That I'm the head of the largest criminal enterprise in the world, that I'm a traitor."

Hallie: "Just focus on staying sober."

Hunter: "You think that I need to apologize to them for the damage I've done through my 'shady' business deals? Thank you again for the support. On this day that Maureen Dowd just fucking skewered me and made me the person that he wins or loses."

Hallie: "You have things all wrong still."

Hunter: "Fuck you fuck you forever fuck you."

Hallie: "Ugh."

By the end of the month, Hunter is moving between hotels in Connecticut, using drugs and ignoring his father's texts.

"Please let me know where you are," Joe writes. "Can I come to see you. Need to talk about 2020 announcement and what you think. I love you."

Joe texts Hunter a few weeks later: "Please call me, Dad."

Hunter: "Is it an emergency."

Joe: "No but important."

In March, Hunter is in a Comfort Inn in Naugatuck.

"Lots brewing with my dad and the shit storm that is about to ensue," he texts a friend. "Presidential campaigns are truly tortuous."

On April 12, Hunter drops off his waterlogged laptop at John Paul Mac Isaac's Mac repair shop in Wilmington, just three miles from Joe's house, and never goes back. He has lit the fuse that could destroy his father's career.

Two weeks later, Joe announces his 2020 candidacy.

Laptop from Hell

"The president is committed to ensuring we have the most ethically vigorous administration in history."
—White House press secretary, Jen Psaki, January 29, 2021

It was just before closing time on a drizzly Friday evening, April 12, 2019, when a disheveled man smelling of booze and cigarettes entered John Paul Mac Isaac's computer repair shop in Wilmington, Delaware. He had three liquid-damaged laptop computers he wanted fixed.

Mac Isaac, a vision-impaired albino man, owned The Mac Shop in the strip mall near Janssen's grocery store. He was a whiz at diagnosing computer problems, and all his Google reviews were five-star. He had no idea what was about to hit him.

One of the laptops his taciturn customer presented was beyond repair. Another had a fried keyboard, so he rummaged around under his counter and found a spare.

The last laptop was salvageable but needed attention. He made out a work order, number 7469, and asked the man his name.

"Biden."

"First name?" he asked.

"Hunter," said the man, irritation in his voice.

Hunter Biden signed the work order with his trademark loopy scrawl and provided a phone number and email address. His signature later would be confirmed as a match with his signatures on other documents.

That night Mac Isaac, forty-four, began the process of recovering the contents of the waterlogged laptop. He called Hunter the next day and asked him to bring in an external hard drive.

Hunter brought the hard drive, and Isaac told him he would extract the contents of his laptop and call him when it was ready.

But Hunter never set foot in the store again.

Mac Isaac made a number of attempts to contact him to pick up his property and pay the $85 bill. No reply.

After ninety days, as per the work order signed by Hunter, the laptop and its contents were deemed "abandoned" and became Mac Isaac's legal property.

In August, Mac Isaac, a Republican voter, heard news reports about a leaked phone call in which President Donald Trump had asked Ukraine's president to investigate Hunter and Joe Biden's involvement with the energy company Burisma. This was the call that sparked Trump's impeachment.

The name "Burisma" rang a bell with Mac Isaac, who had spent hours extracting the contents of the laptop. The hardware was so damaged it needed constant rebooting, and as a result he'd kept a close eye on the data stream.

He did a word search for "Burisma." Bingo. He began to read the emails and documents that popped up.

He sought advice from his father, Steve Mac Isaac, a retired US Air Force colonel. They decided his dad should take a copy of the hard drive to an FBI field office in Albuquerque, New Mexico. But he was turned away without handing over the material.

In mid-October, the FBI phoned Colonel Mac Isaac to ask about Hunter's laptop, and then an agent visited his son in Delaware, to discuss the concerns he had.

On December 9, 2019, Delaware FBI agents Joshua Williams and Mike Dzielak arrived at The Mac Shop with a subpoena and took away the laptop and hard drive. Mac Isaac kept a copy of the material to protect himself.

In January 2020, the impeachment trial against Trump began in the Senate, while a new virus from China quietly bubbled though the country.

The more Mac Isaac watched the trial, the more he believed the Burisma material on the laptop was relevant. He wondered why the FBI was sitting on it. In February he started trying to contact Republican members of Congress, such as Sen. Lindsey Graham and Rep. Jim Jordan, but no one responded.

In August, he saw Rudy Giuliani on TV speaking about Burisma, so as a last resort, he reached out via an email address he found online.

This is the email Mac Isaac wrote, with the subject line "Hunter Biden, on August 27, 2020: "I own and operate The Mac Shop in Wilmington Delaware. Hunter came into my shop on April 12th 2019 and commissioned me to recover data from his macbook pro.

"I recovered the contents of his Mac to my store server and he dropped off an external drive to transfer everything back.

"He never stepped foot in the shop again.

"After repeated attempt to collect payment and to return his property I waited until the 90 day abandonment time period expired and started to go thru the drive and see what was on it....

"As I read deeper into the drive I started to realize what I was sitting on and who was involved and at what level. I figured the safest thing to do was to reach out to the FBI and have them collect the drive and the mac so I could wash my hands of it and they might be able to offer me some level of protection should someone come looking for it and come after me because I knew what was on it.

"The FBI did show up and...over the next few days they contacted me for help in accessing the drive and cable related questions because their tech guy didn't know macs.

"That kinda threw up a flag....

"They also said that nothing ever happens to people that don't talk about this stuff.

"So that got me a little concerned.... There is some very incriminating videos on the drive....

"I live and work in Wilmington, Delaware, and my life here, as well as my business, would be destroyed if people found out what I was involved in.

"I have been trying to keep things quiet...but I feel time has been running out."

Giuliani's attorney, Bob Costello, who used to vet the large volume of messages that flooded the former mayor's inbox, found Mac Isaac's email intriguing.

A blunt character with a mind like a steel trap, Costello was Giuliani's first student assistant in the Southern District of New York in the summer of 1971 and became deputy chief of the Criminal Division.

He could spot authenticity a mile off.

Within two days, he had the hard drive Fed-Exed to his home in Long Island and, with the assistance of his tech-savvy son Bobby, started accessing the data.

(In this book, the words "laptop" and "hard drive" are used interchangeably. A hard drive is a data storage device inside a laptop computer that stores all its digital content. Hard drives also are portable external devices that can be plugged into a computer for use as extra storage or to back up the contents. Mac Isaac made an exact replica of the contents of Hunter's damaged laptop and transferred it onto an external hard drive about the size of a cigarette packet. This was a full image backup of Hunter's laptop—the operating system, boot information, apps, hidden files, preferences, settings, photos, videos, music, emails, calendar, desktop, and so on. In other words, when that hard drive is plugged into another laptop, it is exactly the same as if you are looking at Hunter's laptop. It is like a brain transplant.)

For more than three weeks, Costello performed a forensic deep dive of the hard drive and began the process of verifying the material. He and Giuliani used their law enforcement knowledge to identify multiple alleged crimes in the data they uncovered.

In late September, they consulted Steve Bannon, Trump's 2016 campaign strategist, whose knowledge of CCP power dynamics helped identify Hunter's China connections.

＊＊＊＊

It was Yom Kippur, September 25, 2020, the Day of Atonement. According to Jewish tradition, God inscribes each person's fate for the coming year into a book.

Emma-Jo Morris, the *New York Post*'s twenty-seven-year-old deputy political editor, was at home fasting, in observation of her Jewish faith, when a text came through from an old friend, Vish Burra, producer of Bannon's influential *War Room* podcast.

"Bannon is going to call you. You have to pick up the phone."

A shambolic naval officer turned investment banker, Bannon, sixty-six, was the intellectual leader of the populist nationalist movement that had propelled Trump to victory in 2016. He always turned up at the center of intrigues.

"I have a story that's going to change your life forever," Bannon told her when he called a few minutes later. "I have Hunter Biden's computer."

It was five weeks to the presidential election, in the middle of the pandemic that had upended Trump's cruise to victory.

The first presidential debate was in two nights. Bannon pressed Morris, a former Hannity producer, to promise the front page for debate day.

"You need to chill," she laughed. "There are many more steps we have to take before we would even think about going to print."

Over the course of the next few days, it became evident that Bannon did not have the laptop.

Morris told her editor she smelled a rat. Why would the son of a presidential candidate abandon a laptop with incriminating material on it?

"If you guys are fucking with me I'm going to kill you," she told Burra.

"Look, it's simple," he said. "You grew up in a nice neighborhood. I grew up in Queens with crackheads. This is a crackhead move. He left his laptop and we have it. Just go look at it."

The only person with the hard drive at that stage was Costello, and he was keeping it tight. On September 30, Morris took a one-hour Uber ride to Long Island, where he showed her the incriminating emails and documents he had identified in a month of forensic digging. He allowed her to download some of the most significant material onto a thumb drive.

The *Post* began the painstaking work of independently verifying the material and checking dates of messages with Hunter and Joe Biden's schedules.

There was no doubt it was a bombshell, but the decision about publishing such a strange and explosive story, days before the election, now headed toward the lawyers.

Costello and Giuliani were impatient. The second presidential debate was slated for October 15, and they wanted the story to run beforehand.

Then Trump contracted COVID and was admitted to hospital. Time was running out. They resolved to give the story to another media outlet.

But before they did, Giuliani told Costello: "Call Miranda."

That was how I came to receive Costello's text messages late Friday night, October 9.

After several revelatory conversations the next day with Costello and Giuliani about the evidence they had of Biden family corruption, I texted three images to the *Post*'s senior editorial advisor, Col Allan, the former editor in chief who had brought me to the paper the previous year.

"Huge. Hard drive. 20k emails and pix."

"Call you shortly," he replied.

The lion-hearted, Australian-born Allan, Rupert Murdoch's longest-serving editor, knew a good story when he saw one.

The next day the *Post* was all in. Reporters were hitting the phones and knocking on doors. A photographer headed to The Mac Shop in Delaware for pictures of the FBI subpoena and Hunter's signature on the work order.

The editors insisted the *Post* must have the entire hard drive before publication. Morris issued an ultimatum to Giuliani: "You wanna give selective bits to the *Daily Mail* or Breitbart and get a sloppy job done, be my guest, but we're not doing this unless it's done right."

That afternoon, she was sitting in Giuliani's Upper East Side apartment waiting for a copy of the hard drive. A young woman ushered her into the study, where Giuliani offered her a whiskey. Bannon walked in a few minutes later. "Welcome to the seventh circle of hell," he said as he sat down.

On Wednesday, October 14, the *New York Post* published the first of a series of exclusive stories from the laptop—a 2015 email from Burisma executive Vadym Pozharskyi thanking Hunter for introducing him to the vice president. The email put the lie to Joe's claim he did not know about his son's overseas business dealings.

"BIDEN SECRET E-MAILS. Revealed: Ukrainian exec thanked Hunter Biden for 'opportunity to meet' veep dad," read the front page.

The online exclusive was posted at 5:00 a.m. and was trending all morning on social media platforms.

Six hours later, Facebook pulled the plug. Communications manager Andy Stone, a former Democratic Party operative, issued a statement via Twitter at 11:10 a.m.: "While I will intentionally not link to the *New York Post*, I want be [*sic*] clear that this story is eligible to be fact checked by Facebook's third-party fact checking partners. In the meantime, we are reducing its distribution on our platform."

Twitter followed suit, preventing the story being shared on its platform, on the pretext that it violated rules against "distribution of hacked material." The *Post*'s Twitter account remained locked for two weeks, until election eve.

This was unprecedented, coordinated censorship by two of the largest multinational companies in the world.

After the election, Twitter CEO Jack Dorsey admitted the censorship was a "mistake" and acknowledged the laptop was not "hacked material." Facebook never even bothered to reveal the results of its supposed fact-check.

But the social media suppression had done its job. It had a chilling effect on other media outlets, which dismissed the evidence as "debunked" or "hacked" or just ignored it.

At his morning news meeting on the day the *Post* story broke, CNN boss Jeff Zucker and political director David Chalian instructed staff to disparage it, according to a leaked recording released by undercover news outlet Project Veritas.

"Obviously, we're not going with the *New York Post* story right now on Hunter Biden," said Chalian. "We'll just continue to report out this is the very stuff that the president was impeached over...that Senate committees looked at and found nothing wrong in Joe Biden's interactions with Ukrainians."

At a news meeting two days later Zucker dismissed the story as "the Breitbart, *New York Post*, Fox News rabbit hole of Hunter Biden."

The killer blow came five days after the *Post*'s exposé, from fifty former senior intelligence officials led by the former Obama administration's CIA director, John Brennan, and director of National Intelligence, James Clapper.

Using the institutional weight of their powerful former roles, they signed an open letter—delivered to Politico by former Brennan aide Nick Shapiro—which claimed the material on the hard drive, "has all the classic earmarks of a Russian information operation," although not one of them had seen it.

"We want to emphasize that we do not know if the emails, provided to The New York Post by President Trump's personal attorney Rudy Giuliani, are genuine or not and that we do not have evidence of Russian involvement," the October 19 letter reads. But "there are a number of factors that make us suspicious of Russian involvement.

"Such an operation would be consistent with Russian objectives, as outlined publicly and recently by the Intelligence Community, to create political chaos in the United States and to deepen political divisions here but also to undermine the candidacy of former Vice President Biden and thereby help the candidacy of President Trump....

"A 'laptop op' fits the bill, as the publication of the emails are clearly designed to discredit Biden."

Based as it was on zero evidence, the letter can only be seen as partisan political propaganda designed to disparage the *Post*'s reporting and dissuade the media from looking deeper into the laptop.

It was a curious intervention, considering that the intelligence agencies must have known all about Hunter's international exploits, but their knowledge—and complicity—was a strong motive to suppress the *Post* story.

The Secret Service traveled everywhere with Hunter in the early days. He had the sort of access to the inner sanctums of power in China and Russia any spy would kill for.

Here was someone for whom life had no boundaries. No indulgence was too gross, no perversion was taboo, there was no risk he wouldn't take, no rule he couldn't break with impunity. He recorded every sordid, banal moment of his life as if he were afraid that he would not exist otherwise.

Yet Hunter always seemed to reach the edge without falling into the abyss, as if he had an invisible guardian angel watching over him, even after he declined Secret Service protection from mid-2014.

The drug-addled son of the vice president surely was monitored by US agencies, in ways that few people will ever fully know, if only to protect him from himself.

In any case, the Brennan letter was a lifeline to Joe Biden, coming as it did three days before his final debate on October 22, against a fired-up President Trump.

"If this stuff is true about Russia, Ukraine, China…then he's a corrupt politician," growled Trump. "Joe, they're calling you a corrupt politician. Take a look at the laptop from hell."

Joe relied entirely on the Brennan letter to deflect Trump's attack.

"There are 50 former national intelligence folks who said that what he's accusing me of is a Russian plan. They have said this is, has all the—four, five former heads of the CIA, both parties, say what he's saying is a bunch of garbage. Nobody believes it except him and his good friend Rudy Giuliani."

Trump retorted: "This is where he's going. The laptop is 'Russia, Russia, Russia'? You have to be kidding. Here we go again with Russia."

"You know who he is," Joe told the audience. "You know his character. You know my character. You know my reputation is for honor and telling the truth…."

"The character of the country is on the ballot."

In the hands of Biden campaign operatives, the Brennan letter was a lethal weapon against the *Post*'s reporting, enabling them to dismiss the damning material on the laptop as a Kremlin smear, while never addressing it directly.

They fanned out across the media until Election Day, whenever the laptop was mentioned, always hammering the same message.

Democrat House chairman, Adam Schiff, declared the *Post*'s stories were a smear "from the Kremlin."

Brennan spoke to the favorite mouthpiece of anonymous CIA leakers, the *Washington Post*'s David Ignatius: "There are a lot of issues related to this *New York Post* story that reportedly referenced the Hunter Biden emails, and as I and several of my former colleagues have pointed out publicly, it does bear the hallmarks of Russian disinformation."

Clapper told CNN the laptop was "textbook Soviet Russian tradecraft."

The Brennan letter, in all the glory of its ersatz authority, was the ultimate get-out-of-jail-free card for the Bidens at a time of peril.

Hunter was still leaning on it, months later, while promoting his book on a Daily Beast podcast.

Host Molly Jong-Fast asked him the sharpest questions of his book tour, quoting from incriminating emails on the laptop.

His defense was the Brennan letter: "I don't spend a lot of time on it but there is an intelligence report from all of our intelligence agencies that has come to the conclusion that this was a Russian operation from the get-go."

The letter gave the rest of the media an excuse not to treat the evidence on the laptop seriously.

"We don't want to waste our time on stories that are not really stories," declared National Public Radio managing editor Terence Samuel. "We don't want to waste the listeners' and readers' time on stories that are just pure distractions."

Meanwhile, Joe went to ground for three days after the *Post*'s bombshell. He emerged to fly to Detroit for a closed campaign event and, that evening, briefly stopped for media questions at the airport.

"Mr. Biden, what is your response to the *New York Post*'s story about your son, sir," asked CBS reporter Bo Erickson.

"I know you'd ask it. I have no response. It's another smear campaign. Right up your alley," Biden snarled.

The Biden campaign did not deny the emails were genuine, but backgrounded reporters to say there was no meeting with any Burisma executive listed in Joe's "official" VP diary.

In the days after the *Post*'s exposé, Google searches for "change my vote" spiked, since an unprecedented number of Americans had voted early due to the pandemic. But it is not possible to change a vote once it has been recorded.

We know from polls that, if the full story of the Biden family's foreign influence-peddling scheme had been allowed to be told before the election, it likely would have changed votes.

Almost 50 percent of Biden voters polled after the election knew nothing about Hunter's laptop, according to polling by the Media Research Center, and almost 10 percent said they would not have voted for Joe had they known.

The difference in the battleground states of Arizona, Georgia, Michigan, North Carolina, Nevada, Pennsylvania, and Wisconsin might have swung the election.

With fewer than 45,000 votes in three states deciding the outcome, it's not unreasonable to say that suppression of the *Post*'s Hunter Biden story amounted to election interference.

After he discovered what was on the laptop, Mac Isaac feared for his life, he confided in Bob Costello. He worried when he walked home at night that his poor vision made him more vulnerable to attack.

Wilmington was a Biden town, and he knew it was only a matter of time before people found out what he had done.

It took enormous courage to come forward with evidence of the corruption he had found, but it tore his life apart.

Violent threats forced him to close his thriving business and move to another state. He sued Twitter for defamation, claiming that its "specific intent" in locking down the *Post*'s account was to "communicate to its users…that [Mac Isaac] is a hacker and/or hacked the published materials."

Hunter's former psychiatrist Keith Ablow's life also was thrown into turmoil when the Drug Enforcement Administration raided his Newburyport, Massachusetts, office in February 2020.

Ablow was never charged over the raid, but agents seized a second laptop belonging to Hunter that they found locked in a safe in the basement.

Hunter had left it behind the previous February, and just as he had done in Delaware, he ignored repeated messages to pick it up.

A third laptop belonging to Hunter went missing during a debauched two-week bender in Las Vegas, in August 2018, the year he frittered away as much of his Chinese earnings as he could.

He claimed the computer was stolen by Russian drug dealers and thought they might use it to blackmail him. At the time, he was staying in a $10,000-a-night penthouse suite at the Palms Casino Resort with a pool that jutted out over the edge of the building.

While partying with the Russians, he overdosed and almost drowned.

This, at least, is the story he told six months later to a different Russian, a prostitute, after a sex session filmed on another MacBook in a hotel room.

"I spent fucking crazy amounts of money [when] I went to Las Vegas," he tells her.

"And so literally, after 18 days going round from penthouse suite to penthouse suite [at] four different hotels, and thousands of dollars, I didn't even know [the Russian] had my credit card. He said we got half off. I was like, great. Then I found out it was $10,000 a night. I'm like, what?"

Hunter suggested that he had been drugged because, uncharacteristically, he had passed out, and ended up floating unconscious in the elevated glass pool, high above the lights of Vegas. The anecdote is just one example of the jeopardy in which Hunter placed himself, time and again.

"I went out to the hot tub by myself, which hangs over the edge of the fucking top floor, with glass, it's ridiculous. I'm sitting there and that's the last I remember. And I don't ever pass out, ever.

"I wake up and the only people that are there are Miguel, the guy frantically running round gathering things up, ok...and Pierce, this guy, his friend....

"They had kicked everybody out and they had cleaned up the entire place, and they were getting ready to leave, and I woke up.

"And there was this Russian 35-year-old, really nice...brunette.... She refused to leave.... And they wouldn't call an ambulance, and they didn't know whether I was dead or not, at first. At first I wasn't breathing. I was in the fucking pool face down. They dont know how long...

"Anyway, my computer.... It was fucking crazy shit. And somebody stole it during that period of time. He did all this kind of like pretend search and shit.

"I think he's the one that stole my computer. I think the three of them...the dealer and his two guys. I took them everywhere. Fucking everywhere, crazy out of your mind shit. They have videos of me doing crazy fucking sex."

The prostitute reassures him that, if the videos were going to be leaked, it would have happened already.

But Hunter says: "No, no, no, because my dad [is] running for president. He is, he is, he is. I talk about it all the time…. [The Russians] also know I make like a gazillion dollars.'"

She asks: "They'd try to blackmail you?"

Hunter: "Yeah in some way yeah."

The photo on the cover of this book was taken on that trip to Vegas the previous summer. It was his second day at the Palm, August 3, 2018.

He drove there from Los Angeles in his Porsche the previous day. A photo of the dashboard shows he was speeding at 175 mph on the Las Vegas Freeway in Jean, Nevada, at 12:19 a.m.

By 2:00 p.m. he was ensconced at the Palms and had ordered an enormous room service feast with waffles, soup, and pizza into which he flopped his penis and photographed it.

The same day, he emailed his Wells Fargo wealth adviser and told him to transfer $96,000 to Uncle Jim.

Later that night he texted with a prostitute listed as "Cheryl Vegas" on his phone.

"Honestly babe the problem is you have too many girls there," she writes. "Understand you like a lot of girls but that's fine. Do one at a time—at the tops two, which is fine but just hire the second girl for like an hour…. Sorry I'm not trying to tell you what to do here. But I like you…and you're right, people taking advantage."

He replied: "I do want you to come over but with me it's not an either/or for who stays and who goes. This is not some game of 'Survivor.'"

<hr />

Not long after he dropped off his laptop at Mac Isaac's store, Hunter flew back to L.A. and booked into Petit Ermitage, a boutique hotel in West Hollywood. There he continued his debauched ways until he found himself on a blind date with beautiful South African filmmaker Melissa Cohen, thirty-two.

They fell instantly in love. She took him home, tossed out his drugs, confiscated his laptop, and "nursed me back to life," he wrote in his memoir. Seven days later, they were married.

Later they moved to Malibu with their baby boy, Beau Jr., in a $20,000-a-month rental with an art studio where Hunter cooked up a new grift. He blew blobs of paint through a straw onto white canvases and put them up for sale to anonymous buyers in a New York art gallery for as much as $500,000.

Behind the scenes, federal authorities hadn't been entirely inactive. The securities fraud unit in the Southern District of New York started scrutinizing Hunter's finances in 2019, in the wake of Devon Archer's legal shenanigans, Politico reported.

In Delaware and Washington, DC, investigators also were quietly looking into Hunter over allegations of money laundering and problematic financial ties to foreigners. Uncle Jim was under federal criminal investigation in the Western District of Pennsylvania.

Not that anyone is holding their breath.

When his father won the presidential election in November 2020, Hunter felt enormous relief.

"A Trump victory was not only a threat to democracy [but] it also seemed a threat to my personal freedom," he wrote in his memoir. "If Dad hadn't won, I'm certain Trump would have continued to pursue me."

He was "100 percent certain" that the Department of Justice investigation into his finances would clear him of wrongdoing. And if not, there was always Dad's pardon power.

Four days after the election, Hunter strolled on stage with Joe to declare victory at a socially distanced "car rally" in Wilmington. He gave his father a proprietorial man-hug before surveying the scene with satisfaction, as if it were evidence of his invincibility.

He was back in the bosom of his family, soon to be princeling again in the White House, the president's most trusted adviser, jetting around on Air Force One, the world at his feet.

Just like the old days, only better.

Main Characters

Joe Biden, 79, 46th president of the United States, former vice president

Hunter Biden, 51, the president's son

Kathleen Biden, 52, Hunter's ex-wife

Naomi Biden, 27, Hunter and Kathleen's daughter

Finnegan Biden, 23, Hunter and Kathleen's daughter

Maisy Biden, 21, Hunter and Kathleen's daughter

Beau Biden, 46, Hunter's brother, former Delaware attorney general, died in 2015

Hallie Biden, 48, Beau's widow, Hunter's lover

Natalie Biden, 17, Beau and Hallie's daughter

Hunter Biden II, 15, Beau and Hallie's son

Jill Biden, 70, First Lady, Joe's wife of 44 years

Ashley Biden, 40, Hunter's half-sister, Joe and Jill's only daughter, social worker

Melissa Cohen, 34, Hunter's second wife

Beau Biden, one, Hunter's son with Cohen

Jim Biden, 72, Joe's brother

Valerie Owens, 76, Joe's sister, helped bring up Hunter and Beau

Frank Biden, 68, Joe's brother

Sara Biden, 62, Jim's wife

Caroline Biden, 34, Hunter's cousin, Jim's daughter

Missy Owens, 44, Hunter's cousin, Val's daughter

Casey Owens, 40, Hunter's cousin, Val's daughter

Jean Finnegan Biden, 92, Joe's mother, known as "MomMom," died in 2010

Neilia Hunter Biden, 30, Joe's first wife, Hunter and Beau's mother. Died December 18, 1972.

Naomi Biden, one, Hunter's sister, died December 18, 1972

Lunden Alexis Roberts, 30, former stripper, brought a paternity suit against Hunter

"NJR," three, Roberts' daughter. Paternity test confirmed Hunter is the father

Devon Archer, 48, Hunter's partner, former adviser to Senator John Kerry

Chris Heinz, 48, Hunter and Archer's partner, John Kerry's stepson, Heinz ketchup heir

Tony Bobulinski, 49, Hunter's partner, former US Navy nuclear engineer, CEO of SinoHawk

James Gilliar, 57, Hunter's partner, British businessman based in Czech Republic

Rob Walker, Biden family representative, former Clinton staffer

Jeff Cooper, Biden family benefactor, ran asbestos-litigation firm

Eric Schwerin, Hunter's partner, president of Rosemont Seneca

James Bulger, Hunter's partner, nephew of Boston mobster Whitey Bulger

Michael Lin, 59, Taiwan-born, Beijing-based partner of Bulger

Jonathan Li, Hunter and Archer's partner in Chinese investment fund BHR Partners

George Mesires, 52, Hunter's lawyer, friend.

Keith Ablow, 60, Hunter's friend, psychiatrist

Yelena Baturina, 58, Russian oligarch, widow of former Moscow mayor

Mykola Zlochevsky, 55, Ukrainian oligarch with Russian ties, owner of Burisma

Vadym Pozharskyi, 42, Zlochevsky's lieutenant

Viktor Shokin, 69, Ukraine Prosecutor General, ousted in 2016 under pressure from VP Biden

Ye Jianming, 44, "Chairman Ye," billionaire founder of CEFC. Arrested and vanished in China.

Zang Jianjun, "Director Zang," CEFC director, high-ranking Chinese Communist Party official

Patrick Ho, 72, Ye's lieutenant. Arrested and deported in 2020.

LONGWOOD PUBLIC LIBRARY
800 Middle Country Road
Middle Island, NY 11953
(631) 924-6400
longwoodlibrary.org

LIBRARY HOURS

Monday-Friday	9:30 a.m. - 9:00 p.m.
Saturday	9:30 a.m. - 5:00 p.m.
Sunday (Sept-June)	1:00 p.m. - 5:00 p.m.